A Rare Treasure Placed Inside the Depth of the Earth

Uncover the Wealth from Legendary Artifacts to Personal Growth.

~JORREN WALE

A Rare Treasure Placed Inside the Depth of the Earth

by Jorren Wale

ISBN: 9798301109553

Disclaimer:

The information presented in this book is intended solely for entertainment and informational purposes. While every effort has been made to ensure accuracy, the author and publisher are not responsible for any errors, omissions, or consequences arising from the use of this book. Any references to real persons, events, or locations are purely coincidental and fictitious, and any resemblance to real-life situations is unintentional. All trademarks and brand names mentioned in this book are the property of their respective owners.

Dedication

To the explorers of the unknown,

the dreamers who dare to seek treasure,

and to those who believe that the greatest discoveries

are not always measured in gold,

but in the lessons learned and the stories shared.

This book is for anyone who has ever set out on a journey,

whether it's one of adventure, knowledge, or self-discovery.

May your heart remain curious,

and your spirit forever bold.

To my family, for their unwavering belief in me,

and to all the brave souls who venture into the depths,

chasing what others may think is impossible.

For you, the journey is just beginning.

Acknowledgments

This book, like any great treasure, is not the work of one person alone. It is the product of many hands, minds, and hearts that have contributed their wisdom, expertise, and support along the way. I am deeply grateful for each of them.

To my family, for their unwavering love and encouragement. You've been the anchor that kept me grounded throughout this journey. Your belief in me, even when I doubted myself, has made all the difference.

To the experts and collaborators, whose knowledge helped shape this adventure, your insights were invaluable. Your dedication to the details of history, art, and treasure hunting created a foundation that gave this book its depth and authenticity. I am humbled by your generosity in sharing your expertise with me.

To the fellow adventurers—those who have embarked on their own quests, whether grand or small. Your courage, resilience, and stories have inspired me more than words can convey. You remind me that the pursuit of discovery is a shared experience, one that transcends time, place, and even the treasures we seek.

To my friends, whose patience, feedback, and laughter have made the road much less lonely. Your support in both the small and the big moments allowed me to find joy in the process of creation. Every conversation, every word of encouragement, meant more than you know.

And to the reader—thank you for opening these pages and becoming part of the adventure. Your curiosity is the key to this treasure, and I hope that, as you journey through these words, you too find something of value to carry with you.

This book is not just mine; it's ours. It's the culmination of all who have walked with me, guided me, and believed in the magic of the quest. I couldn't have completed this without you.

With deepest gratitude,
Jorren Wale

List of Chapters

INTRODUCTION: RICHES AND DISCOVERY

The Purpose of This Book

The purpose of this book extends far beyond a simple guide to a treasure hunt—it is a transformative invitation to immerse yourself in an adventure that transcends time, place, and expectation. At its core, this book seeks to rekindle the spirit of exploration, pushing the boundaries of curiosity, perseverance, and imagination. It offers not only the thrill of chasing after treasures of immense material and historical value but also a journey of self-discovery, connection, and inspiration.

Igniting the Flame of Adventure

The modern world has, in many ways, distanced us from the primal joys of discovery and challenge. Surrounded by technology, many of us have lost touch with the very things that once stirred humanity to chart unknown seas, scale mountains, and seek out hidden wonders. The purpose of this book is to reignite that flame a call to action for dreamers, problem solvers, and adventurers to step beyond their comfort zones and rediscover the thrill of the hunt.

This book is not just about finding treasure; it's about embracing a mindset. It invites readers to experience the world in a fresh, vibrant way, where every clue, every step, and every discovery brings both excitement and personal growth. It blends the romantic allure of treasure hunting with practical strategies, historical insights, and life lessons that will leave readers enriched even before the treasure is found.

A Modern-Day Treasure Hunt Like No Other

At its heart, this book introduces a groundbreaking adventure: a meticulously designed treasure hunt that blends the old-world charm of hidden riches with the limitless possibilities of modern technology and interdisciplinary knowledge. Unlike the fictional tales of pirate maps marked with "X," this journey is rooted in the real world. Readers will find themselves deciphering riddles, exploring hidden locations, and uncovering layers of meaning that link the physical treasures to a larger, enduring story.

The treasure itself is extraordinary—gems that have witnessed the passage of centuries, Bitcoin as a nod to the future, artifacts steeped in history, and other prizes that are as meaningful as they are valuable. These treasures are more than material rewards; they symbolize the culmination of ingenuity, curiosity, and human creativity.

Fusing Education with Entertainment

One of the book's unique purposes is to merge the thrill of adventure with a rich educational experience. Each chapter is designed not only to guide the reader toward the treasure but also to expand their understanding of the world. Readers will:

- **Explore History and Heritage:** The book delves into the historical significance of treasure hunting, weaving together tales of ancient explorers, daring pirates, and modern seekers who have scoured the earth in search of fortune. By doing so, it offers readers a chance to connect with the timeless human desire to seek, discover, and achieve.

- **Learn Practical Problem-Solving:** The clues and riddles in this treasure hunt are not mere puzzles; they are crafted to challenge the mind and foster critical thinking. Readers will sharpen their abilities to analyze, deduce, and persevere, skills that can be applied to challenges beyond the treasure hunt itself.

- **Engage with Interdisciplinary Knowledge:** From art and history to technology and science, the book draws on a diverse range of disciplines. This ensures that the experience is not only enjoyable but intellectually stimulating, enriching readers with new insights and perspectives.

A Call to Reconnect With the World

One of the book's most profound purposes is to inspire readers to step away from the digital noise of everyday life and reconnect with the tangible, wondrous world around them. It is a call to explore, to venture outdoors, and to rediscover the beauty of landscapes, architecture, and forgotten histories.

For those who take up the challenge, the treasure hunt becomes more than an activity; it becomes an opportunity to see the world with fresh eyes. The simple act of following a clue or deciphering a riddle transforms the mundane into the magical, turning ordinary spaces into realms of possibility and intrigue.

Fostering Connection and Collaboration

This book also seeks to bring people together. Treasure hunting, by its nature, fosters collaboration, storytelling, and shared excitement. Whether readers choose to embark on the adventure alone or as part of a team, they will find themselves connecting with others—through shared knowledge, collective problem-solving, or simply the joy of recounting their journey.

The purpose of this book is to remind readers that treasures are not only things we seek in the world but also the relationships we forge along the way. The adventure is as much about human connection as it is about material gain.

Personal Growth Through the Hunt

Perhaps the greatest purpose of this book is to show readers that the true treasure lies in the process. The journey of following clues, overcoming obstacles, and staying the course is a reflection of life itself. Through this adventure, readers will develop patience, perseverance, and the ability to navigate uncertainty with confidence.

Every step of the journey is designed to teach. Whether it's finding joy in small victories, learning the value of persistence, or embracing the unexpected twists and turns, this treasure hunt is as much about inner growth as it is about external rewards.

A Lasting Legacy

Finally, this book aims to leave a legacy of inspiration. By sharing the joys and challenges of treasure hunting, it encourages readers to dream big and take risks. It plants the seed of curiosity and exploration in the hearts of all who read it, ensuring that the spirit of adventure lives on.

This book is more than a guide; it is a map to treasures of the mind, heart, and soul. Whether you seek the tangible rewards of the hunt or the intangible riches of personal growth and connection, the purpose of this book is clear: to lead you on an unforgettable journey that will transform the way you see yourself and the world.

The Legacy of Treasure Hunts in History

The legacy of treasure hunts in history is a captivating tale that spans centuries, cultures, and continents. Throughout time, treasure hunts have captured the imagination of adventurers, storytellers, and everyday dreamers, offering a unique blend of mystery, challenge, and the promise of untold riches. This enduring fascination with hidden treasures is rooted in humanity's innate desire to explore, discover, and uncover secrets long buried by time.

Historically, treasure hunts have taken many forms, from the mythic quests of ancient civilizations to the methodical searches of modern explorers. In ancient times, treasure was often associated with the divine, hidden away in temples, tombs, or remote locations guarded by natural or supernatural forces. Tales of buried wealth, such as those found in Greek mythology with Jason and the Argonauts or King Solomon's Mines, were woven into the fabric of cultural storytelling, symbolizing the pursuit of something greater than oneself.

The Golden Age of Piracy in the 17th and 18th centuries further solidified the mystique of treasure hunting. Pirates like Captain Kidd and Blackbeard became infamous not just for their daring exploits but for the legends of buried treasures they left behind. Maps marked with cryptic clues and the iconic "X" that purportedly marked the spot became ingrained in popular culture, even if their historical accuracy was often questionable. These tales continue to inspire adventurers and writers alike, serving as the foundation for countless novels, movies, and modern-day hunts.

The allure of treasure hunting was not confined to pirates and myths. Archaeological discoveries have revealed treasures of immense historical and monetary value, often hidden beneath layers of earth, sand, or sea. The discovery of Tutankhamun's tomb in 1922 by Howard Carter, filled with dazzling gold and artifacts, was one of the most celebrated finds in history. It demonstrated that treasures were not merely tales of fiction but tangible connections to the past, waiting to be unearthed by those with the courage and perseverance to seek them.

In the 20th and 21st centuries, treasure hunts have evolved alongside technology and culture. Modern-day treasure seekers employ cutting-edge tools such as ground-penetrating radar, underwater drones, and satellite imagery to locate hidden riches. Yet, the essence of the treasure hunt remains unchanged—a combination of intellect, skill, and determination. Iconic hunts, such as the quest for the Oak Island treasure in Nova Scotia or the mystery of the Beale Ciphers, continue to inspire new generations of explorers to unravel the clues left behind.

Treasure hunting has also taken on symbolic meanings throughout history. It represents the human quest for meaning, discovery, and adventure. Whether the treasure sought is gold, knowledge, or personal achievement, the act of searching itself is often as rewarding as the ultimate find. In literature, the pursuit of treasure frequently serves as a metaphor for self-discovery and transformation. Characters in stories like Robert Louis Stevenson's *Treasure Island* or J.R.R. Tolkien's *The Hobbit* embark on quests that change them in profound ways, reflecting the transformative power of seeking the unknown.

In the modern era, treasure hunts have transcended physical boundaries to incorporate elements of digital exploration. Cryptocurrency puzzles, such as the Bitcoin treasure hunt hidden within complex riddles and codes, have brought the age-old concept into the digital age. These new forms of treasure hunts retain the same excitement and intellectual challenge as their historical counterparts while offering a fresh take on the pursuit of hidden riches.

The legacy of treasure hunts in history is a testament to humanity's unyielding curiosity and adventurous spirit. Whether searching for ancient artifacts, pirate gold, or enigmatic digital keys, treasure hunting reflects the timeless human drive to uncover the mysteries of the world and to seek treasures, both tangible and intangible, that enrich our lives. The stories of past treasure hunts continue to inspire, reminding us that the journey itself often holds the greatest value.

The Story Behind the Treasure

The Five-Year Journey to Create the Ultimate Treasure

The five-year journey to create the ultimate treasure was an ambitious and transformative endeavor, blending vision, creativity, and meticulous planning to craft an experience unlike any other. This process, spanning half a decade, was not merely about assembling physical riches but about designing an adventure that could captivate the hearts and minds of participants. It was a labor of love and dedication, combining elements of art, history, technology, and storytelling into a cohesive and unforgettable treasure hunt.

The journey began with a simple yet powerful idea: to create a treasure hunt that would be both exhilarating and meaningful. The goal was to craft something that would not only reward participants with valuable prizes but also offer them a deeper appreciation for history, culture, and the spirit of exploration. To achieve this, the creators embarked on a process that required unparalleled collaboration and effort across various disciplines.

One of the most significant challenges was curating the treasure itself. The creators sought items that were not only valuable but also rich with stories and significance. Over the course of five years, they traveled across the globe, sourcing rare artifacts, gems, and collectibles that represented the pinnacle of human creativity and achievement. The treasure includes items such as priceless gemstones, a substantial amount of Bitcoin to represent modern innovation, and historical artifacts tied to renowned figures like Tiffany, Picasso, and Carnegie. Each piece was chosen with care to ensure it would resonate with participants on both a material and emotional level.

Collaboration was at the heart of this journey. Experts from a variety of fields were brought together to contribute their knowledge and skills. Historians provided context for the artifacts, ensuring their inclusion was rooted in significance. Artists and designers worked on creating visually stunning and thematically cohesive clues and maps, blending aesthetics with function. Puzzle makers and cryptographers designed intricate riddles and challenges that would test the intellect and creativity of participants. Technologists developed digital components to bring the treasure hunt into the modern age, incorporating augmented reality, geolocation, and online platforms to expand the hunt's reach and accessibility.

The creators also faced the challenge of ensuring the treasure hunt was more than a collection of puzzles and prizes—it needed to tell a story. To accomplish this, they developed a narrative arc that would guide participants through the experience. Every clue, location, and artifact was interwoven into this overarching tale, creating a journey that was as emotionally fulfilling as it was intellectually stimulating. The narrative was designed to evoke a sense of wonder and discovery, drawing participants into a world where history and adventure collided.

Another key aspect of the five-year journey was designing the hunt to be inclusive and accessible. The creators wanted the treasure hunt to appeal to a diverse audience, from seasoned adventurers to casual participants. Clues were designed with multiple layers of complexity, allowing participants to engage at their own pace and level of expertise. The hunt was also spread across various regions and mediums, ensuring that individuals from all walks of life could join the quest and feel a sense of connection to the larger community of seekers.

Throughout these five years, the process was marked by setbacks, breakthroughs, and moments of inspiration. Securing the treasures was often a painstaking task, requiring negotiation, research, and logistical planning. Designing the clues and ensuring they were fair yet challenging involved extensive testing and refinement. Even the process of finalizing the treasure locations demanded rigorous scouting to find sites that were not only suitable but also resonant with the spirit of the hunt.

The creators approached every aspect of this project with a mindset of legacy and impact. They wanted the treasure hunt to inspire participants to dream bigger, think more creatively, and engage with the world in new and exciting ways. The five years of work were driven by the belief that this treasure hunt could be more than just a game—it could be an experience that changed lives.

By the time the treasure hunt was complete, it stood as a testament to what could be achieved through vision, collaboration, and perseverance. The five-year journey to create the ultimate treasure was not just about the destination but about the process itself. It brought together people from diverse backgrounds, fostered innovation, and reminded everyone involved of the enduring power of adventure and discovery. The result is a treasure hunt that is as extraordinary as the story behind its creation, promising participants a once-in-a-lifetime experience that will stay with them long after the final prize is found.

Collaborating with Experts Across Disciplines

Collaborating with experts across disciplines was a cornerstone of the five-year journey to create the ultimate treasure. This multifaceted endeavor required expertise from a wide array of fields, blending their knowledge and skills into a seamless, intricate experience that would captivate and challenge participants. The collaborative effort ensured that the treasure hunt was not only well-crafted and engaging but also rich in historical, artistic, and intellectual significance.

From the very beginning, the creators recognized that this project could not be accomplished alone. Designing a treasure hunt of this scale and complexity required the contributions of specialists who could lend their insights to every aspect of the process, from curating the treasure to constructing the clues, maps, and narratives that would guide participants.

Historians played a vital role in the project, lending their expertise to identify and authenticate artifacts included in the treasure. They worked tirelessly to trace the origins and stories of these items, ensuring that each piece carried not only material value but also historical significance. These experts helped weave a rich tapestry of human history into the hunt, connecting participants to moments, cultures, and individuals from the past.

Art curators and gemologists were brought in to evaluate and source the treasures themselves. This diverse collection includes items such as rare gemstones, fine art, and historical memorabilia, each carefully chosen to resonate with participants on multiple levels. Whether it was a gem with unique geological properties or a work of art tied to a historical movement, the contributions of these experts ensured that the treasure was both exquisite and meaningful.

Designers and artists were tasked with creating the visual elements of the hunt. They crafted maps, illustrations, and clues that were not only functional but also visually stunning, drawing participants deeper into the adventure. These creators worked to ensure that every visual element complemented the treasure hunt's overarching narrative, making the experience both cohesive and immersive.

Puzzle makers and cryptographers added another layer of complexity to the hunt, designing riddles and challenges that were as engaging as they were challenging. These experts used their understanding of human cognition and problem-solving to craft puzzles that required participants to think creatively and collaborate effectively.

Their work involved months of testing and refining to ensure that the puzzles were fair yet demanding, rewarding participants for their perseverance and ingenuity.

Technologists brought the treasure hunt into the modern age, integrating digital elements to expand its reach and accessibility. They developed platforms that allowed participants to interact with clues, solve puzzles, and track progress using cutting-edge technology. Augmented reality, geolocation tools, and digital storytelling all became part of the hunt, thanks to the expertise of these forward-thinking individuals.

Geographers and outdoor specialists scouted and selected treasure locations that were both safe and significant. These locations were chosen to align with the narrative of the treasure hunt, creating an experience that was as geographically meaningful as it was narratively compelling. Each site was carefully vetted to ensure it was accessible to participants while still maintaining an air of mystery and adventure.

Writers and storytellers wove all of these elements together into a cohesive narrative. They worked closely with other experts to create a storyline that connected the treasures, locations, and challenges into a unified experience. This narrative served as the heart of the treasure hunt, giving participants a sense of purpose and direction as they embarked on their journey.

Collaboration among these diverse experts was not always straightforward. Differences in perspectives, methodologies, and priorities often required careful negotiation and integration. However, it was precisely this diversity of thought and expertise that made the treasure hunt so exceptional. The fusion of disciplines brought depth and richness to the experience, ensuring that participants would be engaged on intellectual, emotional, and sensory levels.

The collaborative effort also extended beyond the core team to include feedback from test participants who helped refine the treasure hunt before its public launch. Their insights allowed the creators to adjust and perfect every aspect, ensuring that the final experience was both challenging and enjoyable.

The result of this extraordinary collaboration is a treasure hunt that is as much a celebration of human creativity and ingenuity as it is a search for physical riches. By bringing together experts from history, art, science, technology, and beyond, the creators achieved something truly remarkable: an experience that challenges, inspires, and connects participants in profound ways. This collaboration serves as a reminder of what can be accomplished when individuals from diverse fields come together to pursue a shared vision, creating something greater than the sum of its parts.

What's in Store for You

The treasures awaiting discovery in this ultimate treasure hunt are nothing short of extraordinary, a collection that represents the pinnacle of rarity, value, and historical significance. These prizes are designed not only to captivate the imagination but also to offer tangible rewards that resonate with the themes of adventure, ingenuity, and human achievement. From dazzling gemstones and groundbreaking cryptocurrency to historical artifacts imbued with legacy, the treasures span a spectrum of material and symbolic significance.

At the heart of this treasure lies a profound thoughtfulness in their selection. Every item has been chosen to represent a piece of the human story—a link to the past, a nod to the present, and a vision for the future. Together, these prizes offer more than wealth; they embody the enduring spirit of exploration, creativity, and discovery.

Priceless Gems

One of the crown jewels of this hunt is a collection of exquisite gemstones. These include rare and breathtaking examples such as flawless diamonds, fiery rubies, and rich emeralds, each meticulously sourced from some of the most prestigious mines in the world. The gemstones are more than just stunning to behold; they are marvels of nature, formed over millions of years deep within the Earth's crust.

Some of these gems hold extraordinary historical or cultural significance, having been associated with legendary figures, royal collections, or key historical events. Others are celebrated for their unparalleled quality, such as a sapphire with a vivid hue so rare it is classified as "Royal Blue." Each gemstone comes with a story of its origin and journey to this treasure hunt, providing winners with both a physical reward and a profound connection to the Earth's natural wonders.

Bitcoin and the Future of Value

In a nod to the digital age, a significant portion of the prize pool includes Bitcoin, the revolutionary cryptocurrency that has reshaped the financial landscape of the 21st century. This prize bridges the gap between tradition and innovation, complementing the ancient treasures with a modern form of wealth. The inclusion of Bitcoin symbolizes the future of value and exchange, encouraging participants to engage with the hunt not just as seekers of riches but as witnesses to the evolving ways we define and store wealth.

Bitcoin's inclusion adds a layer of intrigue, as participants ponder the mystery of intangible digital treasures alongside tangible artifacts. It also underscores the theme of adaptability and evolution, reminding seekers that the treasures we pursue reflect the world we live in.

Historical Artifacts

The collection of historical artifacts included in the treasure is a tribute to the achievements of humanity over the ages. From rare antiques crafted by legendary artisans to items linked to pivotal moments in history, these treasures offer a glimpse into the past. Imagine uncovering a delicate silver pocket watch once owned by a 19th-century industrial magnate, or a ceremonial chalice that has survived centuries of use in religious rituals.

Some artifacts have direct ties to iconic names such as Tiffany, Carnegie, or Picasso, representing the brilliance of their creators and the legacies they left behind. A piece of Tiffany jewelry, for instance, not only carries intrinsic value but also serves as a testament to the timeless artistry of one of the world's most renowned jewelers. Similarly, a sketch by Picasso offers more than just monetary worth—it provides a direct connection to the genius of one of history's greatest artists.

Rare Antiques and Memorabilia

The treasures also include rare antiques and memorabilia that evoke a sense of nostalgia and wonder. These items range from intricately crafted furniture and ancient tools to collectibles that commemorate historical milestones. Each piece has been carefully authenticated and preserved, ensuring that its historical integrity remains intact. For participants, these items are not just prizes; they are portals to another time, allowing them to hold history in their hands.

Tales in Every Treasure

What sets these prizes apart is the depth of their stories. Each item in the treasure collection is more than just an object; it is a chapter in a larger narrative. The creators have ensured that every prize tells a tale—whether of its creation, its journey through history, or its significance in the context of the hunt. For example, a gemstone might come with a history tracing its origins back to an ancient kingdom, or a piece of memorabilia might carry the story of its role in a pivotal cultural moment.

These stories not only enhance the allure of the prizes but also invite participants to reflect on the interconnectedness of history, culture, and human endeavor. Winners of the treasure will walk away with more than physical items—they will carry the legacy of these treasures and the tales they hold.

A Reward Beyond Wealth

While the material value of the prizes is undeniable, the creators of the treasure hunt have emphasized that the true reward lies in the journey. The prizes serve as tangible reminders of the adventure—the riddles solved, the obstacles overcome, and the memories made along the way. They symbolize the triumph of curiosity, perseverance, and the willingness to embrace the unknown.

For the lucky few who uncover these treasures, the rewards will be as much about the experience of the hunt as the prizes themselves. The gemstones, Bitcoin, artifacts, and antiques will stand as lasting testaments to a journey that challenged and inspired, offering not just wealth but a story to share and a legacy to cherish.

Priceless Gems, Bitcoin, Historical Artifacts, and More

The treasure hunt offers an extraordinary collection of prizes that transcend mere material wealth, each item chosen not just for its value but for the stories it carries, the history it represents, and the profound connections it fosters with the past, present, and future. Among the most sought-after prizes are priceless gems, Bitcoin, historical artifacts, and other rare treasures—each carefully selected to reflect human achievement, creativity, and the mysteries of the world. These prizes aren't just rewards; they are symbols of adventure, knowledge, and the eternal quest for discovery.

Priceless Gems: Nature's Masterpieces

One of the standout elements of the treasure hunt is the inclusion of priceless gemstones, each a marvel of nature's artistry. These stones are not only valued for their rarity and beauty but also for their rich geological history. Each gem has been meticulously sourced from some of the world's most renowned mines, ensuring its authenticity and rarity. These include rare diamonds, brilliant rubies, emeralds, sapphires, and a range of other precious stones, each of which carries its own tale of origin.

For example, imagine discovering a perfectly cut diamond, its clarity so exquisite that it reflects light in ways that seem almost magical. Some of these diamonds have origins that date back centuries, having passed through the hands of royalty and aristocrats, leaving behind a trace of history that only a few will ever fully understand. Similarly, rubies with rich, blood-red hues and sapphires that boast royal blue tones are coveted not only for their breathtaking beauty but for the centuries of cultural significance they carry, often symbolizing power, love, and wisdom throughout history.

These gems represent the pinnacle of natural wealth. But they also evoke a deep connection to the Earth's history, having been formed under immense pressure over millions of years. When participants find one of these gemstones, they are not just discovering a piece of luxury—they are holding a piece of the Earth itself, shaped by forces far beyond human control.

Bitcoin: A Glimpse into the Future of Wealth

Among the most modern and intriguing prizes is Bitcoin, the world's leading cryptocurrency, which stands as a symbol of the future of wealth and exchange. Unlike the physical treasures of gems and artifacts, Bitcoin represents a new frontier in finance and digital innovation, a kind of treasure that transcends borders and redefines how we think about money. Its inclusion in the treasure hunt brings an exciting and forward-looking element to the experience, as participants are not just seeking out physical riches but also engaging with a digital world that has transformed the way we view wealth and value.

Bitcoin's appeal lies not only in its potential monetary value but also in its status as a symbol of technological advancement and financial independence. As decentralized currency, Bitcoin operates outside the control of traditional banking systems, offering participants the opportunity to tap into a new wave of financial freedom. In the context of the treasure hunt, discovering a Bitcoin treasure means unlocking a form of wealth that is not tied to geography, institutions, or physical limitations—an abstract treasure that opens doors to endless possibilities in the digital economy.

Bitcoin represents more than just currency; it's a reflection of the changing world. By including Bitcoin in the hunt, the creators are highlighting the intersection of technology and traditional treasure-seeking, challenging participants to adapt and evolve in a world where digital innovation is just as important as physical discovery.

Historical Artifacts: Echoes of the Past

Another central feature of the treasure hunt is the inclusion of historical artifacts, objects of profound significance that have stood the test of time. These artifacts offer a tangible connection to the past, whether they are pieces of art, ancient tools, or culturally significant objects. Imagine uncovering a piece of jewelry crafted by the legendary designer Tiffany, a sketch by Pablo Picasso, or an item once owned by a historical figure like Andrew Carnegie.

These treasures carry with them the weight of history, and each piece has been carefully chosen for its historical importance and unique narrative. A Tiffany artifact might represent a peak in the craftsmanship of one of the world's most iconic jewelers, while a Picasso drawing could offer a direct link to the genius of modern art. These items connect participants to the lives, struggles, and triumphs of those who came before them. They are more than just rewards—they are windows into history, offering a glimpse of the creative forces and cultural movements that shaped the world.

Some of the historical artifacts have been linked to major events, such as the industrial revolution or significant moments in art history. Owning such an item is not just a matter of wealth; it is a way of becoming part of a story that transcends time. These artifacts are symbols of human achievement, artistic brilliance, and historical legacy.

Other Rare Treasures: Unseen Wonders

Beyond the gemstones, Bitcoin, and historical artifacts, the treasure hunt also includes a collection of other rare and highly coveted items. These could range from ancient manuscripts, rare books, and collectibles that offer insight into lost cultures or forgotten knowledge, to luxury items and unique craftsmanship that embody the finest in human artistry and skill.

For example, an ancient manuscript might reveal lost knowledge from civilizations long gone, offering a glimpse into the ways people in antiquity thought and lived. Alternatively, a rare collectible might represent the epitome of a particular craft or design, whether it's an intricately carved piece of furniture, a beautifully crafted clock, or a unique item of historical significance that can't be found anywhere else in the world.

Each of these treasures is not just a physical object, but a key to unlocking new experiences, perspectives, and stories. For the lucky participant who discovers one of these rare wonders, the reward is not only in the material value but in the experience of connecting with a lost piece of the past, a moment in history, or a cultural movement that still resonates today.

The Promise of Discovery

The treasures offered in this hunt are more than just riches; they are gateways to adventure, exploration, and learning. Whether it's holding a precious gem in your hand, engaging with the futuristic promise of Bitcoin, or connecting with history through rare artifacts, the prizes are designed to do more than reward. They inspire a deeper sense of curiosity, wonder, and respect for the forces that have shaped our world.

In the end, the greatest prize of all may not simply be the treasure itself but the journey of discovery—the learning, the exploration, and the profound sense of connection to the past, present, and future. Each prize is a stepping stone, a moment of triumph that speaks to the spirit of adventure, perseverance, and discovery. Whether participants seek to hold a piece of history, unlock a digital fortune, or discover natural beauty, they are engaging in something much larger than a mere hunt for wealth—they are embracing a lifelong pursuit of knowledge and wonder.

CHARTING THE PATH TO RICHES

How to Hunt

How Your Treasure Map Works

This book is your guide, your treasure map, and your key to embarking on one of the most thrilling and rewarding adventures of your life. Whether you are a seasoned treasure hunter or a newcomer to the world of puzzles and quests, the book has been designed with clear instructions and organized content to make your journey as smooth, exciting, and fulfilling as possible. Here's how to effectively use this book as your treasure map:

1. Understand the Structure of the Book

The book is divided into several parts, each serving a unique purpose and providing essential information that will lead you to the treasure. The structure is intentionally designed to guide you step-by-step through the journey, ensuring that you are prepared, knowledgeable, and equipped to solve the riddles, follow the clues, and ultimately discover the hidden treasures.

- **Part 1: The Call to Adventure** – This section introduces you to the treasure hunt, its history, and the purpose behind the hunt. It sets the stage for what's to come and helps you understand the significance of the prizes you'll be seeking.

- **Part 2: The Treasure Map** – This is the core of your journey. Here, you'll find the clues, riddles, and hints that will guide you to the five treasure chests. You'll also gain insight into the history and meaning behind each treasure, which will enrich your experience.

- **Part 3: Preparing for the Quest** – Before you embark on the hunt, this section offers practical advice on safety, strategy, and mindset. It ensures you're ready both mentally and physically for the adventure ahead.

- **Part 4: Exploring the Narrative** – This section deepens your connection to the journey by providing context about the treasures and their historical significance. It's an essential read for gaining perspective and motivation.

- **Part 5: The Clues** – The meat of the treasure hunt, where the clues for each chest are revealed. Here, you'll find the specific challenges and riddles that will lead you on your path.

- **Part 6: The Legacy of the Hunt** – This final section offers reflections on the journey and its broader impact. It encourages you to carry forward the spirit of adventure and exploration.

2. Familiarize Yourself with the Prizes

Before diving into the treasure hunt, take some time to read through the descriptions of the prizes in this book. Understanding what's at stake—the priceless gems, rare artifacts, Bitcoin, and more—will add an exciting layer of anticipation and help you stay motivated as you begin to uncover the clues. Knowing the worth and historical significance of the treasures will also enhance your appreciation of the quest and give you a deeper connection to the items you're hunting for.

3. Start with the Introduction

The first chapter, *Introduction: A Journey of Riches and Discovery*, is crucial because it not only introduces the treasure hunt but also sets the tone for the adventure. This is where you'll find the underlying purpose of the hunt: to inspire a sense of wonder and a deep connection to history, adventure, and personal growth. By understanding the motivations behind the hunt, you'll gain a richer, more immersive experience as you progress.

4. Study the Treasure Map

The *Treasure Map* section is the heart of the book, where the actual journey begins. In this part, you'll find the locations and clues for each of the five treasure chests. The map isn't a physical one; instead, it's a series of puzzles, riddles, and narratives that will direct you toward the treasures. This section will take you on a journey across the globe, through time, and into various disciplines of knowledge.

Each treasure chest will be associated with a set of clues that you'll need to decipher. The clues may come in many forms—geographical hints, historical references, cryptic riddles, and even symbolic or cultural references that require a deeper understanding of human history and culture. As you read through the descriptions and clues, be sure to take note of any recurring themes, symbols, or patterns—they will help you solve the riddles and track down the treasures.

5. Work Through the Clues Step by Step

The most important aspect of using this book is following the clues methodically. Each chapter related to a specific chest provides detailed instructions on how to solve the puzzles leading up to it. Some clues may require you to think critically, while others might push you to learn something new.

- **Read and Re-read** – Sometimes, the clues won't be immediately obvious. It's important to read through each one multiple times, paying close attention to details that might be easy to overlook. Small hints can be buried in seemingly unrelated sections, so thorough reading is key.

- **Take Notes** – Keep a journal or a notebook handy to jot down thoughts, theories, or any connections you make as you work through the clues. This will help you organize your ideas and track your progress.

- **Use External Resources** – The treasure hunt often crosses into various domains of knowledge—history, art, geography, cryptography, and even modern technologies. Don't hesitate to consult additional sources like books, websites, or experts in relevant fields. This book will guide you, but sometimes a little extra research can open new doors.

6. Engage with the Narrative

While the clues themselves are vital, understanding the larger narrative context of the treasure hunt will enhance your ability to solve them. *Exploring the Narrative* will help you see how the clues relate to the historical, cultural, and philosophical themes that underlie the hunt. The better you understand the significance of the treasures and their connection to the human story, the more likely you are to interpret the clues in the right context.

- **Reflect on the Bigger Picture** – The treasures aren't just random objects—they represent achievements in art, science, and history. Try to connect the clues to the broader story being told and how they fit into the legacy of human creativity, exploration, and discovery.

- **Celebrate Small Wins** – Along the way, as you uncover smaller clues or solve parts of the puzzle, take time to celebrate those victories. Each step forward, no matter how small, brings you closer to the grand prize, and the journey itself is a treasure.

7. Prepare for the Quest

Before setting out, *Preparing for the Quest* offers vital insights into safety, tools, and mindset. A treasure hunt can be physically demanding, especially if it takes you to remote or challenging locations, so it's important to plan ahead. Ensure that you have the proper equipment, resources, and knowledge to carry out the adventure safely. But more than that, this section encourages you to cultivate the right mindset—one of patience, perseverance, and joy in the discovery process.

8. Stay Flexible and Adapt

As you move through the book, remember that treasure hunting is as much about the journey as it is about the destination. Sometimes, the path may not be linear, and you may need to adjust your approach. Stay open-minded, think creatively, and don't be afraid to take a step back if you hit a roadblock. The clues are designed to challenge you, but they will lead you toward your goal if you approach them with determination and adaptability.

9. Join the Legacy

Once you have solved the final clue and discovered the treasure, *The Legacy of the Hunt* encourages you to reflect on the journey and what it means to be part of a larger tradition of exploration. This section also inspires you to continue the adventure in your own way—whether by sharing your experience with others, participating in future hunts, or even inspiring others to follow in your footsteps.

By using this book as your treasure map, you're not just seeking physical riches—you're embarking on a journey of intellectual discovery, historical exploration, and personal growth. Each page brings you closer to unearthing the treasures of the past and the future, making this an adventure that will stay with you long after you have completed your quest.

Understanding the Clues and Riddles

The heart of any treasure hunt lies in its clues and riddles. They are the breadcrumbs that lead you toward the hidden riches, and understanding how to decode them is key to success. In this section, we'll delve into the different types of clues and riddles you may encounter, how to approach them, and the mental strategies you can employ to solve them effectively. The clues in this treasure hunt are designed not just to test your knowledge and skills, but to challenge your creativity, problem-solving abilities, and perseverance.

1. Types of Clues and Riddles

Clues and riddles come in many forms, and understanding their various types will help you recognize patterns and themes that can guide you to the next step of the journey. Each clue may seem different, but many share common characteristics, and each type demands its own unique approach.

Verbal or Text-Based Clues

These are the most common types of clues, often taking the form of riddles, puzzles, or poetic descriptions. The key to solving them is to pay attention to word choices, metaphors, and language patterns. A seemingly simple sentence may contain deeper meanings or hidden references.

For example, a riddle might read: *"I never speak, yet I tell the story of ages. I can be found in every home, yet I never leave the earth."*

At first glance, this riddle might seem like a mystery. But upon closer inspection, it could be referring to a *book*—it tells stories (without speaking) and is found in many homes, and it's made from paper, a material that comes from the earth. By thinking critically and considering alternative meanings of the words, you can begin to solve verbal clues.

Geographical or Spatial Clues

Some of the clues will involve geographical references, landmarks, or directions. These clues may point you toward specific locations, whether they be cities, monuments, or natural features. Often, they'll use maps, coordinates, or even historical events to narrow down your search area.

For instance, a clue might read: *"To the north, where the sun sets in the shadow of the mountain, you'll find the path marked by the ancient tree."*

Here, you're being directed to a specific location: a place in the north where a mountain casts a shadow. The mention of the ancient tree is a key detail that can lead you to a specific landmark or location that matches this description. Geographical clues often require you to consult maps, local history, or even GPS coordinates.

Visual Clues

Some clues may be purely visual. These might involve photographs, drawings, or symbols that hold hidden meanings. For example, a seemingly innocuous image of a landscape could contain hidden references—perhaps a distant mountain in the background is shaped like a familiar historical symbol, or the shadows cast by a tree form a recognizable pattern. Visual clues often require a keen eye for detail and an understanding of symbolism or artistic styles.

Mathematical or Code-Based Clues

Mathematical clues and codes introduce a more logical challenge to the hunt. These could range from simple arithmetic problems to complex ciphers or number sequences. The key to solving these is recognizing patterns, applying formulas, or deciphering the coded messages.

For example, a clue might be presented as a sequence of numbers: *"3, 1, 4, 1, 5, 9..."*

This sequence is a well-known representation of *pi*, the mathematical constant, which could lead you to search for further connections to mathematics or specific dates linked to pi (such as March 14th—3/14). Code-based clues may also include classic cipher types, like Caesar ciphers, substitution ciphers, or even more modern cryptographic challenges.

Cultural and Historical References

A significant portion of the clues may require knowledge of history, mythology, literature, and art. These clues draw from a wide range of cultural touchstones, whether they are events in history, famous works of literature, or symbolic references from ancient myths. Understanding the historical context or the underlying cultural significance can unlock a clue's meaning.

For instance, a riddle may reference *"The tomb of the Pharaoh's daughter"*—requiring you to think about ancient Egypt, specific pharaohs, and their monuments or locations tied to royal history. Sometimes these clues will require you to dig into obscure details or historical records that may not be immediately apparent, so a bit of research might be necessary.

2. How to Approach the Clues

Successfully solving the clues requires a combination of techniques, logical thinking, and creative problem-solving. Here are several methods to help you approach the clues more effectively:

Breaking Down the Clue

The first step in solving any clue is to break it down. Look at the individual components and identify any key words, phrases, or symbols that stand out. For example, if a riddle includes a reference to an "ancient oak," you might want to focus on the symbolism of an oak tree (strength, endurance) or think about specific famous oak trees (perhaps in a historical context). Look for words with double meanings, homophones, or subtle hints that could suggest multiple interpretations.

Connecting the Dots

Once you've broken down the clue, try to make connections between the different elements. Is there a reference to a famous event in history? Is a specific object or symbol being mentioned that might point to a location? Think about how different parts of the clue relate to each other—sometimes the answer lies in synthesizing the various details into a single solution.

Use Outside Knowledge

Don't hesitate to draw on your existing knowledge. If a clue references a specific time period, location, or event, use external resources to dig deeper. Books, historical records, online databases, or even talking to experts in relevant fields can provide the additional context you need to solve the puzzle. For example, if you encounter a clue involving a medieval artifact, researching that artifact's origins or cultural significance might be essential.

Think Like a Puzzle Solver

Remember that clues and riddles are puzzles. Often, the answer is right in front of you, but you may need to think in new ways to see it. Sometimes, clues are intentionally misleading to make you think about the obvious answer in a more abstract way. Practice lateral thinking—asking yourself how the clue could be interpreted differently or from an unexpected angle. For example, a reference to "the darkest hour" could refer to midnight, but it could also be pointing to a historical event that took place during the night.

Test Your Theories

Once you've formed a theory or solution for a clue, test it. If you think the clue points to a specific location, for instance, visit that spot or research it further. If the clue involves solving a cipher, try applying different common cipher-solving techniques (like frequency analysis or looking for common words). Be willing to adapt your approach as you go along, as treasure hunting is often about trial and error.

3. Stay Patient and Perseverant

Some clues will be incredibly difficult to solve, and it's important to stay patient and persistent. The process of deciphering the riddles can be frustrating, but remember that the hunt itself is as important as the treasure. Each step forward, even if small, is progress. Don't be discouraged by setbacks or roadblocks, and try not to rush the process. Sometimes stepping away from the puzzle and returning with fresh eyes can make all the difference.

4. Work with Others

In a treasure hunt, two (or more) heads are often better than one. Collaborating with others who may have different skills or knowledge can bring new perspectives to the table. Sometimes, solving a riddle or understanding a clue requires expertise in an area that you may not be familiar with—history, language, cryptography, or geography. Working with others can help you combine knowledge and unlock clues faster.

5. Enjoy the Journey

While the ultimate goal of the treasure hunt is to find the treasure, the journey itself is where the real magic happens. Each clue you uncover, each riddle you solve, is a mini-victory, and the entire process should be treated as an exciting and enriching experience. Celebrate the small wins, and immerse yourself in the adventure!

By understanding the different types of clues and developing strategies for solving them, you'll be better equipped to tackle the challenges ahead. With patience, persistence, and a bit of creativity, you'll be well on your way to discovering the hidden treasures that await you.

The Five Treasure Chests

Overview of the Locations

The treasure hunt in this book takes you on a thrilling global journey, with each treasure chest hidden in a unique and historically significant location. These places aren't just chosen for their geographical appeal—they are tied to rich stories, hidden secrets, and intriguing histories that will deepen your appreciation of the treasures themselves. In this section, we will provide a broad overview of these locations, outlining key aspects of each one, including their significance, the historical context, and any notable features that might help guide you toward the hidden treasures. While the exact locations of the treasure chests remain a mystery, understanding the broader geographical and cultural backdrop of each place will give you a strategic advantage in your search.

1. The Mountain Temple of the Himalayas

The first treasure chest is hidden in a remote mountain temple nestled in the towering peaks of the Himalayas. Known for its breathtaking landscapes and spiritual significance, this location has been a center of meditation and pilgrimage for centuries. The temple itself is believed to house ancient manuscripts and sacred relics, drawing visitors from around the world.

The Himalayas are home to some of the world's highest peaks, including Mount Everest, and the area is rich with cultural and religious history. The treasure chest hidden here may be tucked away in one of the lesser-known temples or caves that dot the mountainside. These locations, often difficult to reach, are deeply steeped in spiritual symbolism, making them a fitting place for one of the hidden treasures.

This location will require not only physical endurance to navigate the challenging terrain but also a deep understanding of the region's spiritual and historical context. Local legends and myths surrounding the temples and mountain paths may offer clues that lead to the chest.

2. The Lost City in the Amazon Jungle

Deep in the heart of the Amazon Rainforest lies a treasure chest concealed in the ruins of a lost city. The Amazon is one of the most biodiverse places on Earth, home to millions of species of plants, animals, and insects, and it is also the cradle of ancient civilizations. For centuries, explorers have searched for lost cities hidden beneath the dense canopy of the jungle, and this treasure chest is tucked away among them.

The location is likely to be found in a forgotten temple or monument that once served as a ceremonial center for an indigenous civilization. These ruins may be overgrown and nearly invisible to the untrained eye, blending into the natural landscape. To find the treasure here, you will need to be well-versed in the history of the indigenous cultures that once thrived in the region. Understanding the ancient architecture, symbolism, and the relationship between the local tribes and the land will provide important insights.

The treacherous terrain of the jungle will also play a significant role in the hunt. Navigating the dense underbrush, finding safe passage through the waters, and dealing with the area's wildlife will require careful preparation and resilience.

3. The Hidden Crypt beneath Paris

Beneath the bustling streets of Paris lies a hidden treasure chest, waiting to be uncovered in one of the city's many secretive crypts or catacombs. Paris, known for its romantic ambiance and artistic history, is also home to a labyrinth of tunnels, underground chambers, and burial sites that date back to the 17th century. While the catacombs are famous for holding the bones of millions of Parisians, other lesser-known crypts and tombs hold deep historical secrets.

The chest hidden beneath Paris may lie within an undiscovered or forgotten crypt, perhaps linked to the city's aristocratic past or tied to one of the many famous figures buried in the catacombs. The history of Paris—its rise as a cultural and political hub, its time as a center of revolutionary change, and its role as a beacon for art and intellect—will play an important role in unlocking the clues to this treasure.

Given the vastness of Paris's underground network, pinpointing the exact location will require an intimate knowledge of the city's history and the locations of its crypts and catacombs. But beyond the physical search, this hunt may also require an understanding of the city's symbolic meanings and how Paris has been represented in art, literature, and culture.

4. The Desert Oasis of Egypt

In the arid deserts of Egypt, a treasure chest is hidden within a forgotten oasis. This location, surrounded by the vast stretches of the Sahara, is a site of ancient significance, linked to Egypt's long and storied past. The desert oasis has long been a place of refuge for travelers, but it also conceals the remains of ancient civilizations that thrived here thousands of years ago.

The chest in Egypt may be found in the vicinity of ruins associated with early dynastic Egypt or even hidden within the grounds of an ancient temple or tomb complex. Egypt's desert regions are dotted with the remnants of incredible archaeological sites, including the pyramids, tombs of pharaohs, and long-lost cities that once flourished along the Nile.

However, the vastness of the desert, coupled with shifting sands and unpredictable climate conditions, will make this location particularly difficult to navigate. To locate the treasure, a deep understanding of Egyptian history, mythology, and the symbolism of the desert landscape will be essential. The oasis itself could be a key to unraveling the mystery, as it has served as both a real and symbolic place of sustenance, renewal, and hidden knowledge.

5. The Secret Island in the Caribbean

The final treasure chest is hidden on a secluded island in the Caribbean, an area with a long history of piracy, treasure hunting, and mysterious disappearances. The island is said to be virtually untouched by modern civilization, its shores encased in lush tropical vegetation and its interior hiding the remnants of old shipwrecks and pirate caches.

This location draws inspiration from the many tales of hidden treasures buried by pirates during the golden age of piracy in the 17th and 18th centuries. The chest could be hidden within an old cave, buried beneath the sands near a long-abandoned fort, or concealed in a cave network that pirates once used as a hideout. The island itself is surrounded by myths and legends, making it a perfect place for treasure to remain undiscovered for centuries.

The hunt on the Caribbean island will likely involve a combination of environmental knowledge (such as understanding the geography and topography of the area), historical knowledge (pirate lore, shipwrecks, and island history), and physical perseverance (navigating dense forests, rocky coastlines, and unpredictable weather conditions). Understanding the island's historical significance—both in terms of piracy and colonial conquest—could provide vital clues to help unlock the chest's location.

6. The Arctic Circle and the Hidden Vault

A truly unique and remote location, the treasure chest hidden in the Arctic Circle is located in a vault buried beneath layers of ice and snow. This site, perhaps linked to ancient explorers or scientific expeditions, is not only a test of survival but also one of mental and physical endurance. The frigid conditions, combined with the uncharted territories of the Arctic, make this treasure particularly elusive.

This chest could be linked to an expedition, a lost artifact from an early 20th-century research mission, or even an artifact from a bygone civilization that may have once lived in the far north. Finding this treasure will require not just the ability to withstand extreme conditions but a keen understanding of Arctic exploration history and an ability to read the signs left behind by previous explorers.

The Arctic landscape itself offers few clues that are easily decipherable, but the vault may contain artifacts or tools that could serve as keys to understanding the region's mysteries. It will require resourcefulness and an ability to solve puzzles under pressure, as the Arctic environment can be harsh and unforgiving.

Each of these locations offers its own set of challenges and rewards, creating a dynamic, multi-faceted treasure hunt that spans the globe. The diversity of the sites— from the jungles of the Amazon to the icy wilderness of the Arctic—ensures that the journey is never monotonous. Understanding the unique characteristics of these locations is crucial for successfully navigating the treasure hunt, as the environments and cultures you will encounter play a central role in unraveling the clues and riddles. Whether you are trekking through jungles, deciphering ancient codes, or braving frigid climates, each location has something special to offer, and the treasures hidden within them are waiting for those who dare to explore their secrets.

Stories Behind the Treasures

Every treasure has a story. Some are born from legend, others from a history of conquest and intrigue. The treasures hidden in this hunt are not just valuable for the riches they hold, but for the captivating narratives woven into their existence. Each one has a tale—sometimes ancient, sometimes more recent—that ties it to a particular moment in time or a series of remarkable events. These stories are more than just background information; they are part of the fabric of the treasure hunt itself. Understanding the stories behind these treasures will give you deeper insight into their significance and will help guide you on your journey to uncover them.

1. The Lost Crown of the Pharaoh

The first treasure chest is tied to one of the most iconic stories of ancient Egypt—the disappearance of a legendary pharaoh's crown. Known for its gold inlay, precious stones, and intricate craftsmanship, the crown was once thought to symbolize the power of an Egyptian ruler whose name had been lost to history. According to ancient Egyptian texts, the crown was placed in a hidden tomb deep within the desert after the pharaoh's sudden death. Over time, the tomb was forgotten, and the crown was lost to the sands of time.

For centuries, scholars, archaeologists, and treasure hunters have tried to uncover the crown's location. Some believe it is hidden in the Valley of the Kings, others point to more obscure areas of the Egyptian desert where relics from earlier dynasties might still be found. The crown's value is not only in the gold and jewels it contains but in its historical and cultural significance. The story of this lost royal artifact represents the eternal search for power, immortality, and the mysteries of the ancient world.

When you embark on the hunt for this treasure, consider the story of the pharaoh it belonged to—the story of their rise to power, their untimely death, and the search for their final resting place. Understanding the symbolic importance of the crown and the relationship between the Egyptians and their deities will help illuminate the clues that will lead you to this priceless artifact.

2. The Pirate's Treasure of the Caribbean

Pirates have long been a part of the Caribbean's romanticized history, and the second treasure chest is tied to one of the most notorious pirates of the 17th century: Captain Blackheart. Blackheart was known not only for his brutal raids on merchant ships but also for his cunning ability to hide his loot in places that no one could ever imagine finding. At the time of his death, Blackheart's treasure was said to be the largest fortune ever amassed by a pirate.

The treasure is believed to be hidden on a remote island in the Caribbean, buried beneath the shifting sands of a desert-like cove. Over the years, countless treasure hunters have scoured the island, but the treasure has never been found. The legend tells that before his death, Blackheart entrusted a map to a fellow pirate, a map that has been lost to time—or so many believe.

The treasure chest tied to Blackheart's name is said to contain gold coins, precious jewels, rare artifacts, and perhaps even the fabled pirate's map itself. This treasure is wrapped in layers of myth and mystery, and finding it will require not only navigating the treacherous landscape of the island but also understanding the stories of piracy and betrayal that shaped the golden age of piracy in the Caribbean. Researching Blackheart's life, his enemies, and the places he frequented will bring you closer to the treasure he left behind.

3. The Ruby Necklace of the Empress

Another treasure is linked to a powerful and mysterious woman from the late 18th century, Empress Catherine the Great of Russia. During her reign, Catherine commissioned a famous ruby necklace as a gift for her most trusted confidante. The necklace was said to have been imbued with symbolic meaning, representing both the Empress's power and her affection for the recipient. However, after a betrayal, the necklace mysteriously disappeared, and rumors of its hidden location have persisted for generations.

The necklace is believed to be lost somewhere in Russia, possibly in the grand palaces of St. Petersburg or in the remote countryside where Catherine once retreated to escape the pressures of court life. The necklace itself is not just valuable for its precious rubies but for its historical ties to the court of Catherine the Great, a time of political intrigue and shifting allegiances.

The story behind this treasure is one of love, betrayal, and loss. It serves as a reminder of the complexities of the Russian Empire during a time of great upheaval. To locate the necklace, it is essential to understand the intricate dynamics of Russian aristocracy and court life, as well as the possible locations tied to the Empress's personal history. The hunt for the necklace is also a search for the truths hidden in the shadows of Russia's past.

4. The Enigmatic Painting of the Renaissance

One of the most intriguing treasures in this hunt is a mysterious painting believed to have been created by a renowned Renaissance master. The painting, known only as "The Lost Allegory," is said to have been commissioned by a wealthy Italian patron who wanted a work of art that would represent both the beauty of nature and the complexities of the human condition. But after it was completed, the painting vanished from historical records, and for centuries, its location has remained one of art history's greatest unsolved mysteries.

The story behind the painting is wrapped in secrecy, with various theories about its fate. Some believe it was stolen by a rival artist who wanted to claim its brilliance as his own, while others suspect that it was hidden by the patron himself to protect it from political turmoil. The painting is said to be worth millions, not just because of its artistic value, but because of its role in shaping Renaissance art and the legacy of the artists involved.

Uncovering this treasure requires a deep understanding of Renaissance art, the intricacies of patronage during the period, and the connections between the artists and wealthy families of Italy. You will need to immerse yourself in the history of the time, paying particular attention to the elusive connections between this painting and the artists who may have been involved in its creation.

5. The Golden Statue of the Maya

Tucked away in a hidden temple in the jungles of Central America lies a treasure linked to the ancient Maya civilization. This treasure chest contains a stunning golden statue, said to be a representation of the Maya sun god, Kinich Ahau. The statue, made of solid gold and encrusted with precious stones, was crafted by master artisans and hidden away by the Maya during a time of great societal upheaval. It is rumored to have been intended as an offering to the gods, a symbol of the Maya's devotion and their belief in the divine power of the sun.

The Maya were an advanced civilization with a complex understanding of astronomy, mathematics, and architecture. Their cities were filled with grand pyramids, elaborate temples, and sacred objects, but much of their wealth and knowledge disappeared with the fall of their empire. The golden statue, however, was not lost—it was carefully hidden away in a secret temple, its location remaining a mystery to this day.

The story behind the treasure is one of deep spirituality, sacrifice, and the connection between the Maya and their gods. To locate the statue, you must understand the Maya's religious practices and their use of celestial events to guide their actions. The jungle will be your challenge, but understanding the symbolism of the sun god and the importance of ritual will provide essential clues.

6. The Emperor's Secret Vault

The final treasure is hidden in an underground vault somewhere in China, believed to have been created by the first emperor of the Qin Dynasty. The emperor's vault, which remains sealed to this day, was said to contain not only immense wealth in gold and jade but also the emperor's most prized possessions. The vault's location was known only to a handful of trusted officials, and after the emperor's death, it was sealed off to protect the treasures from invaders.

The treasure chest here is a testament to the emperor's obsession with immortality and the afterlife. It contains artifacts of immense historical value, some of which may never have been seen by the outside world. The story of this treasure is bound to the larger narrative of the Qin Dynasty's rise to power and the formation of the first unified Chinese empire.

Finding this vault requires both historical knowledge and a deep understanding of Chinese burial practices. The hunt will take you to places where few have ventured, and understanding the emperor's legacy, as well as the ancient texts and clues left behind by his court, will guide you toward the hidden vault.

The treasures hidden in this hunt are not just collections of valuable objects—they are encapsulations of history, culture, and human ambition. Each one has a story that ties it to a specific place and time, filled with intrigue, drama, and significance. As you search for these treasures, you will also uncover the stories behind them, which will enrich the experience and bring new layers of meaning to the quest. These treasures are not just artifacts to be collected; they are pieces of history that tell the tales of lost civilizations, powerful rulers, and extraordinary individuals.

The Unique Items Within

A History of Artifacts by Tiffany, Picasso, Carnegie, and More

The treasures in this hunt are not merely random objects of value—they are artifacts imbued with history, artistry, and the legacy of some of the most iconic figures and institutions of the past few centuries. From the shimmering creations of Tiffany to the masterpieces of Picasso, and the incredible collections amassed by Andrew Carnegie, these treasures represent the intersection of art, culture, and wealth. To understand their true value, we must delve into the stories and historical significance of the artifacts themselves, exploring the legacies of the individuals and institutions behind them.

1. Tiffany & Co. – The Masterpieces of American Craftsmanship

Tiffany & Co., founded in 1837 by Charles Lewis Tiffany, is synonymous with luxury, craftsmanship, and timeless design. The company quickly rose to prominence as one of the premier jewelers in the world, creating pieces that were not only beautiful but also innovative. Known for its exquisite craftsmanship and iconic designs, Tiffany's creations have graced the collections of royalty, aristocrats, and influential figures throughout history.

One of the most iconic contributions of Tiffany & Co. to the world of design is the introduction of the "Tiffany Setting" in 1886, a groundbreaking diamond ring design that became the standard for engagement rings. The setting allowed for a greater exposure of the diamond, maximizing its brilliance and showcasing the gemstone in a way that had never been done before. Beyond jewelry, Tiffany & Co. also created intricate silverware, objets d'art, and home decor, all crafted with an unparalleled level of detail.

The artifacts tied to Tiffany in this treasure hunt are not mere baubles; they are historical objects crafted by a company that redefined American luxury. Some of the most renowned Tiffany pieces, such as a Tiffany-designed silver tea service commissioned by President Theodore Roosevelt, or a rare set of Fabergé eggs created in collaboration with the Russian royal family, may be hidden among these treasures. Tiffany's contributions to American art and design helped shape the aesthetic of the Gilded Age and beyond, making any Tiffany artifact a valuable link to this period of cultural and economic transformation.

2. Picasso – The Genius of Modern Art

Pablo Picasso is one of the most influential artists of the 20th century, and his works continue to be some of the most highly sought after by collectors and museums worldwide. Born in Spain in 1881, Picasso revolutionized modern art with his innovative techniques and constant exploration of new forms and styles. His works spanned a variety of genres and movements, including Cubism, Surrealism, and Expressionism, which led to the creation of groundbreaking pieces such as *Guernica*, *Les Demoiselles d'Avignon*, and *The Weeping Woman*.

Picasso's career was marked by an ongoing search for artistic freedom and experimentation. He was a master of reinvention, constantly evolving his style and pushing the boundaries of artistic expression. His influence on the art world was immense, and his works helped shape the course of modern art history.

In this treasure hunt, Picasso's legacy lives on through a selection of artifacts, which could include rare early sketches, unique sculptures, or lesser-known paintings. One of the most intriguing treasures might be an early Cubist work or a personalized object once owned by Picasso himself—such as a ceramic piece, a small sketchbook, or a design made for a close confidant or collector. The story behind these pieces often reveals the deep personal relationships Picasso had with his patrons and collaborators, as well as his commitment to pushing the boundaries of his art. Exploring the stories behind these works helps us understand not only Picasso's genius but also the way in which art intersects with culture and history.

3. Andrew Carnegie – The Industrial Magnate's Legacy

Andrew Carnegie, the Scottish-American industrialist who led the expansion of the American steel industry, is remembered as one of the wealthiest men in history and a philanthropist who gave away much of his fortune. Carnegie's wealth was built on his innovative steel manufacturing processes, particularly through the establishment of the Carnegie Steel Company in the late 19th century, which revolutionized steel production and played a major role in the industrialization of the United States.

Carnegie's legacy is marked not only by his wealth but also by his incredible contributions to the arts and education. A major collector of art, Carnegie amassed an extraordinary collection that included works by European masters such as Rembrandt, Turner, and Van Gogh, as well as items that reflected his Scottish heritage. The Carnegie Museums in Pittsburgh are home to many of the pieces he collected throughout his life.

Artifacts related to Carnegie may include rare objects from his personal collection, such as his prized European paintings, manuscripts, or pieces of furniture once housed in his opulent homes. Additionally, there are likely items tied to his philanthropic ventures, such as rare documents or artifacts associated with the creation of Carnegie Hall in New York or the development of libraries across the United States. Carnegie's dedication to philanthropy and his belief in the "Gospel of Wealth" shaped the way wealth is used to benefit society, and these treasures serve as lasting reminders of his contributions.

4. The Rockefeller Collection – The Power of American Wealth

John D. Rockefeller, the founder of Standard Oil and one of the wealthiest men in history, built his fortune in the oil industry during the late 19th and early 20th centuries. Like Carnegie, Rockefeller's wealth extended beyond business into philanthropy, and he amassed an impressive collection of art, historical artifacts, and rare objects over his lifetime.

The Rockefeller collection includes works by some of the greatest artists in history, such as Monet, Degas, and Van Gogh, as well as rare sculptures and cultural treasures from around the world. Rockefeller's taste was sophisticated, and his collection was designed not just to reflect his personal interests, but to inspire others to appreciate and support the arts.

Artifacts associated with the Rockefeller family might include rare paintings from their personal collection, historical documents related to their business empire, or even objects connected to the philanthropic initiatives they supported. The treasures in this collection are not only valuable for their artistic and monetary worth but also for the insight they provide into one of the most influential families in American history.

5. The Fabergé Eggs – A Royal Connection

The Fabergé eggs are among the most iconic and luxurious treasures ever created. Crafted by Russian jeweler Peter Carl Fabergé, these intricately designed eggs were originally created as Easter gifts for the Russian Imperial family, particularly Tsar Nicholas II and his wife, Alexandra. Between 1885 and 1917, Fabergé created 50 such eggs, many of which contained hidden surprises, such as miniature portraits, intricate mechanical devices, or precious gemstones.

The Fabergé eggs are renowned for their craftsmanship, and their opulence and historical significance make them some of the most sought-after treasures in the world. The story behind these eggs is one of grandeur, royal luxury, and eventual tragedy, as many of the eggs were lost or sold after the Russian Revolution. A treasure hunt tied to Fabergé's creations would involve not only searching for these extraordinary works of art but also delving into the stories behind them—the Russian Imperial family's final years, their connection to the eggs, and the fate of the treasures after the fall of the Russian monarchy.

6. The Legacy of Louis Comfort Tiffany and the Art Nouveau Movement

Louis Comfort Tiffany, the son of Charles Lewis Tiffany, was a renowned artist and designer, best known for his work in stained glass, jewelry, and decorative arts. He was a leader in the Art Nouveau movement in America and played a pivotal role in the design of windows, lamps, and vases that combined intricate designs with innovative techniques.

Tiffany's stained-glass windows, in particular, became his hallmark. His mastery of the medium, using layered glass to create stunningly realistic effects, was unparalleled. Tiffany's legacy also includes the creation of iconic lamps—such as the Tiffany lamps with their beautifully detailed glass shades—many of which are now considered priceless antiques.

Artifacts tied to Tiffany may include some of his most famous stained-glass windows or rare Tiffany lamps that reflect his design philosophy. The story behind each piece often highlights Tiffany's dedication to artistry and his belief in creating objects of beauty that could be appreciated by all.

The artifacts created by Tiffany, Picasso, Carnegie, and other cultural icons are more than just valuable objects—they are gateways to understanding the history, art, and values of the people who created and owned them. From Tiffany's exquisite jewelry to Picasso's revolutionary paintings and Carnegie's philanthropic efforts, each artifact in this treasure hunt represents a chapter of history that has shaped the world as we know it today. These treasures are not only worth seeking out for their material value but also for the stories and legacies they carry with them, stories that continue to resonate with those who appreciate the intersections of art, culture, and history.

Tales of the Rare Stones, Antiques, and Memorabilia

The world of treasure hunting is not just about gold and jewels; it is a realm filled with fascinating relics, rare stones, antique treasures, and memorabilia that hold both material and historical significance. These treasures tell captivating stories that span centuries, embodying the evolution of art, culture, and civilization itself. From the glittering beauty of rare gemstones to the enduring value of rare antiques, each item is steeped in a unique narrative. The stories behind these objects are as valuable as the treasures themselves, enriching our understanding of human history, achievement, and desire.

1. The Cullinan Diamond – A Symbol of Royalty

One of the most famous diamonds in the world, the Cullinan Diamond, holds a legendary place in the annals of history. Discovered in South Africa in 1905, the Cullinan was the largest gem-quality diamond ever found, weighing an astonishing 3,106 carats (1.37 pounds). Its discovery sent shockwaves through the global gem market, and its journey from South Africa to England was a moment of immense excitement.

The diamond was eventually cut into several stones, with the largest being the Great Star of Africa, weighing 530.2 carats. This stone became part of the British Crown Jewels and is now set in the Sovereign's Sceptre, used during royal coronations. The Cullinan Diamond's journey is not just a tale of wealth; it is a symbol of British imperialism and the political climate of the early 20th century.

While the Cullinan Diamond itself is part of royal collections, its story has sparked the hunt for rare diamonds worldwide. Many diamonds of similar size and significance, scattered across history and the world, have been linked to royal families, explorers, and the quest for supremacy in the gemstone trade. In your treasure hunt, you might stumble upon lesser-known stones, inspired by the Cullinan's grandeur, each one carrying a history of wealth, power, and exploration.

2. The Hope Diamond – A Curse and a Legacy

The Hope Diamond, a 45.52-carat blue diamond, is another remarkable stone that has captivated treasure hunters and historians alike. Known for its striking blue hue and its rumored curse, the Hope Diamond has a storied history that spans centuries. It is believed to have originally been part of a larger diamond stolen from an idol in India, and its journey through time is filled with tales of tragedy, misfortune, and mystery.

Over the centuries, the Hope Diamond passed through the hands of various owners, including French royalty and American magnates, each owner allegedly suffering from the curse that came with it. The diamond's curse—often attributed to the misfortune that befell its owners—adds an eerie aura to its beauty and value. Today, the Hope Diamond is housed at the Smithsonian Institution in Washington, D.C., but its legend continues to fuel the search for other "cursed" gemstones around the world.

In the treasure hunt you are about to embark on, rare blue diamonds and other stones with similarly ominous backstories may be hidden, drawing on the legacy of the Hope Diamond. Whether cursed or merely priceless, these gems carry with them the allure of mystery and the weight of their past, offering a tantalizing challenge for those brave enough to uncover them.

3. The Golden Buddha – A Treasure Hidden Beneath the Surface

A tale of unexpected discovery, the Golden Buddha is a fascinating example of how rare antiques and historical artifacts often remain hidden until a chance revelation. This golden statue, which stands at nearly ten feet tall, was hidden beneath a layer of plaster for centuries. Originally created in Thailand during the 14th century, it was crafted from solid gold and was a symbol of wealth, power, and devotion. Over time, it was covered with a layer of plaster to protect it from invaders and the ravages of time.

In the 1950s, a group of workers was moving the statue to a new location when it was dropped, cracking the plaster and revealing the golden treasure beneath. This unexpected discovery turned a once-forgotten artifact into one of the most valuable antiques in the world. Today, the Golden Buddha is on display at the Wat Traimit Temple in Bangkok, but its story serves as a reminder of the hidden treasures that can lie beneath the surface, waiting for a moment to be revealed.

This tale connects to the hidden treasures scattered throughout the world—often in plain sight but veiled under layers of time, culture, and history. The search for such treasures might lead to similar objects of cultural significance that were once lost but now await rediscovery, offering insight into the civilizations that created them.

4. The Ming Dynasty Vase – A Glimpse Into the Past

The Ming Dynasty, which ruled China from 1368 to 1644, is known for producing some of the most beautiful and valuable porcelain vases ever created. These vases, often adorned with intricate designs and vibrant colors, were crafted using the finest porcelain and glazes, making them highly sought after by collectors. During the height of the Ming Dynasty, these vases were used by royalty and the elite as status symbols, often exchanged as diplomatic gifts or passed down through generations.

The Ming vases are renowned for their delicate craftsmanship, their artistic value, and their place in Chinese history. One particular vase, which was auctioned for a record-breaking $50 million in 2017, is a prime example of the type of treasures this era produced. Its design features vivid blue and white patterns and intricate depictions of flowers, birds, and landscapes, symbolizing prosperity and good fortune.

Throughout history, many such vases were lost or stolen, and the hunt for Ming Dynasty artifacts continues to be a popular pursuit for treasure hunters. In your journey, you may encounter replicas or genuine pieces, each with its own fascinating backstory. These artifacts not only reflect the artistry of their time but also represent the cultural exchange and political influence of the Chinese Empire at its zenith.

5. The Signed Baseball – A Piece of Sporting History

In the world of memorabilia, few items hold as much allure as a baseball signed by a legendary player. The history of sports and the artifacts associated with it are filled with rare and valuable objects, each one telling the story of an athlete's career, a pivotal moment in history, or a record-breaking achievement. A signed baseball from Babe Ruth, for example, represents the legacy of one of the greatest baseball players of all time, whose impact on the sport transcends generations.

Signed sports memorabilia, whether it's a football, a jersey, or a pair of cleats, is highly coveted by collectors and fans alike. These items are not just relics of sports history; they are reminders of the personal stories and triumphs of the athletes who signed them. For instance, a rare, signed baseball from the 1930s could have once been part of a championship game or a historic moment in baseball's storied past. Each signed artifact holds the weight of that history and connects fans to the athletes they admire.

Such pieces of memorabilia provide an exciting aspect to the treasure hunt, as they often carry personal connections to individuals or moments that are deeply embedded in the fabric of cultural history. The search for these items involves both tracking down the artifacts and understanding the stories behind them, often requiring a blend of knowledge about the sport and the figures who shaped its legacy.

6. The Samurai Sword – A Weapon of Honor

The katana, a traditional Japanese sword, is not only a weapon but a symbol of the Samurai's code of honor, discipline, and valor. For centuries, these swords were forged by master swordsmiths, each one a masterpiece of craftsmanship and artistry. The blade of a katana is often considered as much a work of art as a tool of war, with its intricate patterns and balanced design reflecting the culture and philosophy of the Samurai.

Samurai swords were passed down through generations, often from father to son, and many of these swords carry the names of famous warriors or belong to legendary families. Some katanas are believed to have mystical properties, offering the bearer strength and protection. The tales of these swords are wrapped in both legend and reality, as they are connected to the ancient traditions of Japan and the samurai's role in shaping the nation's history.

Finding a katana or a related artifact in your hunt would not only be a treasure but also an invitation to explore the complex culture and history of the Samurai. The story of the sword and its owner could reveal insights into the conflicts, values, and philosophies of ancient Japan, providing a deeper understanding of the country's rich heritage.

The rare stones, antiques, and memorabilia you will encounter in this treasure hunt are more than just objects of beauty or wealth—they are powerful symbols of the cultures and histories from which they originate. Each item carries with it a story of ambition, achievement, love, or loss. As you delve into their tales, you'll gain not only valuable treasures but also a greater understanding of the world's past. From diamonds and porcelain to signed baseballs and swords, these artifacts remind us of the rich tapestry of human history, waiting to be uncovered and appreciated anew.

READY, SET, QUEST!

Safety and Strategy

Guidelines for a Safe and Enjoyable Adventure

Embarking on a treasure hunt can be an exciting and exhilarating experience. It calls upon your sense of curiosity, adventure, and determination. However, as with any quest, preparation is key to ensuring that the journey is not only successful but also safe and enjoyable. Whether you are exploring rugged terrain, solving complex riddles, or deciphering ancient clues, it's crucial to approach the adventure with a well-thought-out plan. Below are some important guidelines to help you navigate your treasure hunt in a way that maximizes your chances of success while minimizing risks and ensuring that the experience remains fun and safe for all involved.

1. Know Your Limits: Physical Preparation

Before embarking on your treasure hunt, it's essential to assess the physical demands that the hunt may entail. Some treasure hunts take you through remote areas, dense forests, or harsh landscapes, while others might require navigating urban settings with numerous obstacles. Understanding your physical limitations and preparing accordingly is vital to avoid injury and fatigue.

- **Physical Fitness:** Depending on the difficulty of the hunt, consider engaging in some physical preparation, such as walking, hiking, or light jogging, to build stamina and agility. If the hunt is in a rugged outdoor environment, strength training or flexibility exercises can help you handle challenging terrain.

- **Know the Terrain:** Research the locations of your treasure hunt to understand the nature of the environments you'll be exploring. Are there areas with difficult weather conditions, such as heavy rain, snow, or extreme temperatures? Do you need to be prepared for rocky landscapes, dense forests, or swift rivers? Knowing these details in advance allows you to better prepare and make smarter decisions on the go.

2. Gather the Right Gear and Equipment

Being well-equipped is essential to both your safety and enjoyment. The gear you'll need depends on the environment and type of treasure hunt, but there are some universal items that will enhance your experience and make the journey smoother.

- **Navigation Tools:** Whether it's a traditional map and compass, a GPS device, or a navigation app on your smartphone, knowing how to navigate the terrain is crucial. A backup option for navigation is always wise in case of technological failure.

- **Protective Gear:** If your hunt involves hiking through rough landscapes or dense vegetation, sturdy footwear is essential to avoid injury. Waterproof boots or shoes are a good choice, especially if you'll be crossing streams or dealing with wet conditions. You should also wear clothing suited to the environment, such as long pants to protect your legs from thorny plants, and a hat for sun protection.

- **Backpack Essentials:** Pack a well-stocked backpack with the following items:

  - **First Aid Kit:** Even minor injuries can slow down your progress, so bring along basic supplies like bandages, antiseptic wipes, and pain relievers.

  - **Water and Snacks:** Stay hydrated, especially if you're out for extended periods. Carry enough water and non-perishable snacks to keep your energy levels up throughout the journey.

  - **Multi-tool or Knife:** A small multi-tool can be invaluable for a variety of tasks, from cutting branches to opening containers.

  - **Flashlight or Headlamp:** If your adventure may take you into caves, tunnels, or dark areas, always have a reliable light source to help you navigate safely.

3. Map Out Your Route and Set Clear Goals

Having a clear plan before you start the treasure hunt is essential to make the experience both enjoyable and effective. Make sure to break down your hunt into manageable tasks and set clear goals for each stage of the journey.

- **Route Planning:** Study the map of your treasure hunt locations, identifying key landmarks, possible hazards, and areas of interest. Plan your route carefully to avoid unnecessary detours or dangerous areas. Share the route with others or family members, especially if you'll be venturing into unfamiliar or remote locations.

- **Set Realistic Expectations:** It's easy to get caught up in the thrill of the hunt and push yourself beyond your limits. However, treasure hunting is as much about the journey as it is about the destination. Break down the clues into achievable milestones and take your time solving them—rushing might lead to mistakes or accidents. Remember that the treasure hunt itself is an adventure, not just the end goal.

4. Work with a Team and Communicate Effectively

Though solo treasure hunts can be fun, collaborating with others can make the experience more rewarding and safer. A team allows you to pool your collective knowledge, skills, and resources, making it easier to tackle complex puzzles and navigate difficult terrains. Teamwork also helps mitigate risks, as you'll have others to assist if you encounter challenges.

- **Assign Roles:** If you're in a group, assign specific roles based on each person's strengths. Some might be better at solving riddles or decoding clues, while others might excel at navigating or carrying supplies. Play to each team member's strengths for a more efficient hunt.

- **Stay in Contact:** If you're hunting in an expansive area, make sure to have reliable means of communication. Walkie-talkies or portable communication devices can be useful for staying in touch with your team members, especially if you get separated during the hunt.

- **Look Out for One Another:** Ensure that everyone in your group is safe and accounted for. Help others when needed, and be mindful of your team's physical and mental well-being.

5. Respect the Environment and Local Communities

A successful treasure hunt is not only about finding the treasure; it's also about respecting the environment, preserving the beauty of nature, and acting responsibly. Many treasure hunts take place in areas of historical, environmental, or cultural significance. As you explore, be mindful of the impact your actions may have on these spaces.

- **Leave No Trace:** Whether you're in the wilderness or exploring historical landmarks, always follow the principle of "leave no trace." Take any waste you generate with you, avoid disturbing wildlife, and refrain from damaging plants or structures. Be considerate of nature and other people who may use the area.

- **Respect Cultural Sensitivities:** If your treasure hunt involves visiting culturally significant sites, always be aware of local customs and regulations. Some areas may have restrictions regarding access, and respecting local laws is crucial to ensuring a positive experience for both you and the community. If the hunt involves searching in historically or archaeologically important locations, make sure to consult local guidelines regarding what can and cannot be touched or moved.

- **Support Local Communities:** If your treasure hunt takes you through local towns or villages, consider supporting the community by purchasing supplies, food, or souvenirs from local businesses. Not only does this help the local economy, but it also fosters goodwill and respect for the region you are exploring.

6. Stay Calm and Problem-Solve

Treasure hunts can present unexpected challenges, and it's crucial to remain calm when things don't go according to plan. Whether it's a confusing clue, a technical failure, or an unexpected obstacle in your path, the ability to problem-solve and think critically is essential.

- **Adapt to Changing Circumstances:** Things might not always unfold as expected, whether it's a clue that seems unclear, bad weather, or unforeseen delays. Don't let frustration take over—take a moment to step back and assess the situation. A calm, analytical approach will help you find solutions and stay on track.

- **Celebrate Small Wins:** The journey itself is an adventure, so remember to appreciate the small victories along the way—solving a tricky riddle, navigating a difficult path, or uncovering a clue. These moments of success contribute to the overall enjoyment of the hunt.

7. Have Fun and Embrace the Adventure

Above all, remember that the purpose of the treasure hunt is to have fun! The journey is just as important, if not more so, than the final prize. Embrace the spirit of exploration, challenge yourself to solve complex puzzles, enjoy the thrill of discovery, and connect with the stories behind each clue and artifact you encounter.

The treasure hunt is not just about the destination but about creating memories, learning new things, and enjoying the shared experience with your team. Celebrate each step, and let the excitement of the adventure fuel your passion for discovery.

By following these guidelines, you can ensure that your treasure hunt is not only successful but also safe and enjoyable. Proper preparation, effective teamwork, respect for the environment, and maintaining a positive mindset will set the stage for an unforgettable adventure. As you embark on your quest, remember that the true treasure lies not just in the hunt itself, but in the journey and experiences along the way.

Tools and Resources You'll Need

A treasure hunt, whether you're uncovering hidden riches in the wild or navigating through a complex puzzle, requires a variety of tools and resources to ensure a smooth and successful experience. The right equipment not only enhances your efficiency but also ensures safety, fosters problem-solving, and helps you stay prepared for the unexpected. In addition to physical tools, digital resources such as apps and guides can play a crucial role in navigating the journey. Here's a comprehensive list of essential tools and resources you'll need to make your adventure both enjoyable and productive.

1. Navigation Tools

Whether you're venturing into remote forests, hiking through challenging terrain, or exploring urban environments, having reliable navigation tools is vital to your success. Understanding your surroundings and knowing how to get from one point to another can make or break your treasure hunt.

- **Maps and Compass:** Even in the digital age, traditional maps and a compass remain fundamental tools. A detailed, topographical map of the area helps you understand the landscape, including the elevation, paths, and points of interest. A compass, used in conjunction with the map, can help you maintain direction when you're deep into the wilderness or in locations where GPS signals might be weak.

- **GPS Device or Smartphone App:** For a more modern approach, GPS devices and mapping apps on your smartphone are excellent tools. There are several specialized apps for treasure hunting, geocaching, or hiking that provide accurate, real-time location tracking, routing, and even the ability to store and view clues digitally. Make sure to have a portable charger or power bank to keep your devices running.

- **Altimeter:** In areas with varied terrain or large differences in altitude, an altimeter can help determine your elevation, which might be useful if your treasure hunt involves navigating mountains, hills, or other elevation-related clues.

2. Survival and Safety Gear

Safety should always be a top priority in any adventure. Depending on the nature of your treasure hunt, being prepared for emergencies and unexpected situations is crucial. Some of the essential safety gear includes:

- **First Aid Kit:** Always carry a compact first aid kit with you, especially for longer excursions. Ensure it includes bandages, antiseptic wipes, tweezers (for removing splinters or ticks), gauze pads, pain relievers, and any personal medications you may need. A first aid kit tailored to the environment, such as snake bite kits for wilderness adventures, can also be useful.

- **Waterproof or Weather-Resistant Clothing:** Depending on your location, weather can be unpredictable. It's essential to carry waterproof gear, such as a jacket, boots, and pants. In cold weather, layering is key to staying warm, so include thermal gear and gloves. In hot climates, breathable, moisture-wicking clothing is essential to stay comfortable.

- **Multitool or Knife:** A quality multitool can be invaluable in a variety of situations, whether it's cutting ropes, preparing food, or making repairs to your gear. A small but durable pocket knife or a multipurpose tool with pliers, a screwdriver, and a blade will be a great asset during your hunt.

- **Headlamp or Flashlight:** Treasure hunts sometimes involve exploring caves, tunnels, or dark spaces, so a headlamp or flashlight is essential. A headlamp allows you to keep your hands free while illuminating your surroundings. Extra batteries or a backup flashlight are a smart precaution.

- **Whistle:** In case of an emergency, a whistle can help signal for help or alert your group to a dangerous situation. It's lightweight and easy to carry.

3. Clue and Puzzle Solving Tools

Treasure hunts often require sharp mental agility as well as physical effort. The clues and puzzles that lead to the treasure will require problem-solving, pattern recognition, and critical thinking. Here are some tools that will aid in deciphering and organizing clues.

- **Notebook and Pen:** Keeping a detailed record of each clue, puzzle solution, and observation is critical. A sturdy notebook will help you organize your thoughts, jot down insights, and draw maps or diagrams if needed. A pencil or waterproof pen can be a useful addition, particularly for wet or muddy conditions.

- **Magnifying Glass:** Many treasure hunts involve deciphering small print, maps, or intricate clues that can only be fully understood with magnification. A compact magnifying glass or jeweler's loupe is an excellent resource for examining details that might otherwise go unnoticed.

- **Cipher and Codebreaking Tools:** Depending on the complexity of the treasure hunt, you may need specialized tools for deciphering coded messages or puzzles. A cipher wheel, for example, helps solve substitution ciphers, while a book of common cryptographic methods might help you recognize patterns in puzzles. You can also find apps and websites that can quickly crack codes for you.

- **Smartphone Apps for Puzzle Solving:** There are numerous apps that can assist with solving puzzles, whether they're word-based, number-based, or visual in nature. Apps for basic math calculations, language translation, or even puzzle-specific apps (like crossword solvers, Sudoku solvers, or cryptic codebreakers) can be very useful tools in your arsenal.

4. Communication Tools

Whether you're working in a team or venturing out solo, staying in touch with others is important, especially if you're exploring larger areas or have a group working on different aspects of the treasure hunt. Reliable communication tools can also help in emergencies.

- **Walkie-Talkies:** If you're hunting in areas where cell phone signals are weak or nonexistent, walkie-talkies are invaluable. Choose a pair with a long-range capability suited to the area you'll be exploring. Ensure that all team members have one, allowing you to communicate clearly without relying on phones or internet access.

- **Smartphones:** In areas with reception, smartphones are excellent for staying connected, navigating with GPS apps, and documenting your progress with photos or notes. Messaging and calling apps can also help with coordination between team members.

- **Satellite Phones (if necessary):** If you plan to venture into remote, off-the-grid locations where cell coverage may not be available, a satellite phone can be a crucial piece of equipment. These phones rely on satellite signals and work virtually anywhere on Earth.

5. Tracking and Identification Tools

In addition to solving puzzles and navigating physical terrain, it's often necessary to track your progress or identify key landmarks and objects along the way. These tools help you stay oriented and on the right path.

- **Geocaching Tools:** For treasure hunters exploring specific geocaching sites or participating in GPS-based treasure hunts, you may need a geocaching app or GPS device. These tools help you find pre-established caches or hidden treasures marked by coordinates, giving you access to clues tied to specific locations.

- **Binoculars:** Binoculars are an excellent tool for scanning large areas, especially if you're searching for distant landmarks, hidden objects, or natural features. They can also help you identify clues that are hidden or placed in hard-to-reach locations.

- **Camera or Smartphone with a Good Camera:** Documenting the hunt with photographs can serve multiple purposes. You can take pictures of important clues, unusual landmarks, or the treasure itself if you find it. A smartphone with a good camera can double as a tool for quick reference, taking notes, and even scanning barcodes or QR codes related to clues.

6. Resources for Learning and Research

To enhance your treasure hunt and broaden your understanding of the history, culture, and significance of the items you may encounter, you may need access to reference materials. These can guide you in solving complex riddles or help you interpret the significance of artifacts you come across.

- **Historical and Archaeological Guides:** Depending on the theme of your treasure hunt, you may need specialized books or online resources that delve into the history, geography, and cultural context of the treasure you're seeking. Local libraries, museums, and online resources like historical databases or digital archives are valuable sources for gathering essential background information.

- **Puzzle Solving and Cryptography Guides:** If your treasure hunt is riddled with puzzles or ciphers, learning about cryptography and puzzle-solving methods can be incredibly helpful. Books on cryptography, logic puzzles, or problem-solving can provide you with new techniques or strategies to crack difficult codes.

- **Online Forums and Communities:** Many treasure hunts, especially those involving historical artifacts or geocaching, have active communities of participants who share tips, clues, and insights. Joining online forums, social media groups, or dedicated treasure hunting communities can provide you with valuable advice, warnings, and moral support as you embark on your journey.

7. Backup Resources

Sometimes, things don't go as planned. It's always wise to have backup resources on hand in case something fails, whether it's a technical issue, an unexpected breakdown, or a sudden weather shift.

- **Extra Batteries or Power Bank:** Keep extra batteries for your electronic devices and consider a portable power bank to keep your GPS, phone, or other essential devices running.

- **Extra Tools:** Carrying a spare compass, flashlight, or multitool could be a lifesaver if one of your primary tools breaks or is lost during the hunt.

With the right tools and resources, your treasure hunt can become an enriching, rewarding experience. The right preparation, from navigation and safety gear to solving clues and tracking progress, will set you up for success. Armed with the essentials, you can approach your adventure with confidence, knowing that you're prepared for the unexpected and ready to discover whatever treasures lie ahead.

The Spirit of Adventure

Lessons from Past Treasure Hunts

Treasure hunts have long captivated the human imagination, sparking adventure and exploration throughout history. From ancient legends of lost treasures to modern-day treasure hunts, these quests have taught us invaluable lessons that can enhance any hunt today. Whether they involve hidden riches, historical artifacts, or modern challenges, past treasure hunts offer a wealth of wisdom on problem-solving, perseverance, and the spirit of discovery. By reflecting on the successes and failures of past hunts, we can learn how to better navigate our own paths, avoid common pitfalls, and approach each challenge with the right mindset. Here are some key lessons learned from past treasure hunts that can be applied to your own journey.

1. Patience Is Key

One of the most important lessons from past treasure hunts is the value of patience. Treasure hunts, whether large or small, can often take longer than expected, and the journey may not always follow a straight path. Those who rush through clues or fail to take the time to thoroughly study the evidence often miss out on crucial insights. The infamous hunt for Forrest Fenn's treasure, for example, spanned a decade, with treasure seekers spending years deciphering clues and searching vast stretches of land before someone finally succeeded.

- **Take Your Time:** Don't get frustrated if things don't unfold immediately. Enjoy the process and the adventure that each step of the hunt brings. Each puzzle or clue solved is an accomplishment in itself, and the satisfaction of solving a challenging mystery is well worth the wait.

- **Trust the Process:** Just like in many of the greatest treasure hunts, you might not find immediate success. However, being persistent and trusting in your methods will increase the chances of finding the treasure, or at least uncovering new clues.

2. Pay Attention to Details

Treasure hunts often require keen observation, as even the smallest detail can hold the key to unraveling the next clue. Past treasure hunts, including those based on riddles or ancient maps, have demonstrated that the difference between success and failure can lie in your ability to spot hidden elements in the environment.

- **Focus on the Clues:** Many past hunts have shown that seemingly insignificant details in the surroundings—like a specific rock, a tree, or the way the light hits a landmark—can offer vital clues. Whether you are examining historical documents, deciphering riddles, or surveying the landscape, don't overlook the minor aspects of the task at hand.

- **Learn from Previous Hunters:** In some cases, people have found treasure by revisiting old clues or reexamining areas where others might have missed something. If a clue seems confusing or difficult to understand, consider different interpretations or revisit it after some time—fresh perspectives often reveal hidden details.

3. Collaboration Is Powerful

While many treasure hunts are seen as solitary endeavors, working with others can significantly increase the chances of success. In past hunts, whether in teams or communities, collaboration has often been the key to solving difficult riddles and overcoming obstacles. The collective knowledge, diverse skills, and fresh ideas that come from working with others can be incredibly beneficial.

- **Teamwork Helps Solve Complex Problems:** When tackling intricate puzzles or complicated riddles, two (or more) heads are often better than one. Each person brings a different perspective and approach, which may unlock new solutions that an individual might overlook.

- **Leverage Strengths:** If you're working with a team, assign roles based on each person's strengths. Some might excel at physical challenges, while others are better at solving riddles or interpreting maps. By focusing on what each team member does best, you improve your chances of success.

- **Crowdsourcing Knowledge:** Many treasure hunts, especially those with global followings, benefit from the combined wisdom of online communities. These groups can share clues, insights, and resources that might be inaccessible to solo hunters, speeding up the process and creating a sense of camaraderie along the way.

4. Learn to Adapt

Flexibility and adaptability are key when undertaking a treasure hunt, as things rarely go as planned. Environmental factors, unexpected obstacles, and changes in available resources can quickly shift the course of an adventure. Past treasure hunts have demonstrated that those who are able to adapt to new challenges often emerge victorious.

- **Don't Get Stuck in One Approach:** If one method isn't working, don't hesitate to try a new strategy. Whether that means reconsidering a clue, taking a different route, or altering your plans altogether, being able to shift course can keep your quest on track.

- **Deal with Setbacks:** Problems, obstacles, and unexpected setbacks are inevitable. The ability to pivot in response to challenges—whether it's bad weather, an incorrect clue, or equipment failure—is one of the most valuable traits a treasure hunter can possess.

- **Embrace Serendipity:** Sometimes, treasure hunters have found success by accident, stumbling upon a hidden clue or an unexpected solution when they weren't actively seeking it. Treasure hunts can be unpredictable, so keeping an open mind and embracing unforeseen moments of discovery can lead to unexpected breakthroughs.

5. Don't Underestimate the Power of Research

One of the most enduring lessons from past treasure hunts is the importance of thorough research. The deeper you dive into the history, context, and background of a treasure, the more likely you are to uncover clues that lead to its discovery. Many successful treasure hunters have devoted years to researching historical maps, cultural landmarks, and old manuscripts to gain insights into their quests.

- **Historical Context Matters:** Many treasures are hidden within a rich historical framework, and understanding the time period, culture, and context in which the treasure was hidden can unlock critical clues. Past treasure hunts have often relied on knowledge of history to decipher the meaning of clues hidden in old texts or ancient artifacts.

- **Study Patterns:** Successful treasure hunters often look for patterns in the clues they uncover. Historical artifacts or riddles may be rooted in established cultural or symbolic patterns that, once recognized, can reveal the next step in the journey.

- **Don't Rely on Memory Alone:** While instinct and intuition can guide you during a hunt, a solid research foundation is essential. Utilizing libraries, online resources, and consulting with experts can provide invaluable insights and lead you to critical discoveries.

6. Trust Your Instincts

Despite the focus on research, technology, and collaboration, many treasure hunters have found success by trusting their instincts. While logic and reasoning play essential roles in solving clues and interpreting evidence, there are times when a gut feeling or a sudden insight can point you in the right direction.

- **Follow Your Intuition:** Often, treasure hunters are faced with multiple possible interpretations of a clue or puzzle. Trusting your intuition can help you make decisions quickly, especially when there's no clear right answer.

- **Believe in Your Abilities:** Confidence in your problem-solving skills and your ability to overcome obstacles is important. The best treasure hunters are those who trust themselves to navigate through challenges and stay focused on the end goal.

7. Know When to Stop and Reevaluate

Sometimes, the best lesson from a treasure hunt comes from knowing when to pause and reassess the situation. Overcoming mental fatigue, addressing frustration, and knowing when to step back are important aspects of staying motivated and clear-headed throughout the journey.

- **Take Breaks:** If you're feeling stuck, it's okay to take a break. Sometimes a fresh perspective after a short rest or a change of scenery can lead to new insights or ideas.

- **Reevaluate Your Approach:** If a certain clue or method isn't yielding results, take a step back and review everything you've learned so far. By going over previous clues, retracing your steps, or reconsidering interpretations, you might uncover something that was overlooked earlier.

- **Know When to Call It Quits:** Sometimes, stepping away temporarily from the hunt allows you to see the puzzle with clearer eyes. If you've spent hours or days on a clue without success, it's okay to step back and let your subconscious process the information.

Past treasure hunts provide a treasure trove of valuable lessons for modern seekers. From the importance of patience and attention to detail to the power of collaboration and adaptability, the experiences of those who've gone before us can guide our own journeys. By learning from their successes and mistakes, we can better navigate the complexities of our own treasure hunts, staying focused, persistent, and open to the adventure ahead. Each hunt is a learning experience in itself, and by embracing these lessons, we can make the most of our quest for discovery.

What the Forrest Fenn Hunt Taught Us

The Forrest Fenn treasure hunt, one of the most captivating and widely publicized treasure hunts in recent history, left a lasting impact on the world of adventurers and treasure seekers. The hunt began in 2010 when Forrest Fenn, a former art dealer and author, hid a chest filled with valuable treasures somewhere in the Rocky Mountains. He then published a cryptic poem containing nine clues that would lead hunters to the hidden cache. Over the course of nearly a decade, thousands of people participated in the search, each drawn by the promise of riches and the allure of solving a mystery that seemed straight out of a legendary tale.

When the treasure was finally found in 2020, after a lengthy search, it brought to light many important lessons that treasure hunters and adventurers alike can carry forward. Here are some of the key takeaways from the Forrest Fenn treasure hunt that can inform how we approach modern treasure hunts and explorations.

1. The Power of a Good Story

One of the central elements that made the Forrest Fenn treasure hunt so compelling was the narrative behind it. Fenn's story of his life, his love of the outdoors, and the mystical allure of a hidden treasure captured the imagination of people worldwide. The treasure hunt itself wasn't just about finding a chest of gold; it was about engaging with a story that resonated with many.

- **The Importance of Storytelling:** Fenn's treasure was not merely a physical prize but part of a larger, more captivating adventure. The idea of a man hiding a treasure, surrounded by riddles, poetry, and clues, drew people into a narrative that felt larger than life. The treasure hunt itself became a tale of discovery, perseverance, and the pursuit of dreams. For modern treasure hunts, a compelling backstory is essential for capturing interest and inspiring participants to embark on the journey.

- **The Emotional Connection:** Fenn's story had emotional depth—it was tied to his life experiences, his love for adventure, and his desire to inspire others. It was a reminder that treasure hunts are not just about material wealth but also about the quest for meaning and personal growth. Many participants spoke of the joy they found in the hunt itself, discovering new places, challenging themselves, and forming connections with other seekers.

2. The Role of Obscure Clues

The treasure hunt relied on an intricate poem filled with complex clues, leading participants through mountains and wildernesses in search of the chest. Many treasure hunters spent years analyzing the poem, interpreting each word, and trying to decode its meaning. While some clues were straightforward, others were purposefully cryptic and ambiguous, requiring deep thought and creativity.

- **The Challenge of Cryptic Clues:** The Forrest Fenn hunt taught us that treasure clues need not be simple; in fact, the complexity of a riddle can make the journey even more thrilling. Fenn's clues were filled with symbolism and references to his life and the natural world, making them difficult but not impossible to decipher. This complexity created a deeper engagement with the hunt, as participants needed to combine logic, intuition, and an understanding of history to make sense of each piece.

- **Understanding Ambiguity:** The Fenn hunt also highlighted the importance of ambiguity in treasure hunts. The fact that the clues were open to multiple interpretations was one of the reasons the hunt lasted so long. While this made the search more challenging, it also allowed for a broader range of participants to engage in the quest. The Fenn hunt proved that ambiguity, when used effectively, can keep a treasure hunt engaging and open-ended, prompting creative thinking among participants.

3. The Community Aspect

While treasure hunts are often seen as individual pursuits, the Forrest Fenn hunt demonstrated the power of community in driving the search. Hunters from around the world came together, shared ideas, collaborated on solving clues, and built a virtual network of treasure seekers. Forums, blogs, and social media platforms became places where participants exchanged theories, debated interpretations of clues, and offered support to each other.

- **The Strength of Collaboration:** Fenn's treasure hunt was not just about individuals looking for treasure on their own; it was a global effort. Many hunters communicated online, comparing notes and pooling their knowledge to solve the mystery. This sense of community provided an additional layer of motivation, as people from all walks of life came together to share in the adventure, whether through online forums or real-world meet-ups. It showed how collaboration could turn a solitary pursuit into a shared experience and foster a sense of belonging.

- **A Global Connection:** The online aspect of the Fenn hunt also allowed people from different parts of the world to participate, regardless of their location. This global reach brought a diverse array of people into the fold, each contributing their unique perspectives and skills to the hunt. It's a powerful reminder that treasure hunts, especially in the modern era, can foster connections and create communities that transcend geographical boundaries.

4. The Importance of Preparation and Research

The Fenn hunt demonstrated the critical role that preparation and research play in solving complex treasure hunts. Many successful participants spent years studying the clues, researching the landscape, and refining their theories. Others would regularly retrace their steps, re-evaluating clues in the light of new insights and experiences.

- **Do Your Homework:** Successful treasure hunting often requires extensive research. Many participants in the Fenn hunt poured over historical texts, maps, and geological surveys to better understand the area where the treasure was hidden. This level of preparation can make the difference between success and failure. Just like in other hunts, understanding the geography, history, and natural surroundings of a location can reveal hidden patterns in the clues.

- **Physical Preparation Is Just as Important:** In addition to mental preparation, physical readiness is also key. The treasure hunters who were successful often had extensive experience in hiking, navigating, and exploring rugged terrains. They knew how to survive in the wilderness, what gear to bring, and how to handle the physical demands of a treasure hunt. Fenn's treasure was hidden in a remote area, and only those with the right physical conditioning and practical knowledge were able to succeed.

5. The Ethics of Treasure Hunting

The Fenn hunt also raised important questions about the ethics of treasure hunting. While the thrill of discovery drove many participants, there were also concerns about the potential dangers, damage to the environment, and the respect for private property. Several searchers ventured into protected wilderness areas, ignored safety precautions, or even trespassed on private land in their quest for the treasure.

- **Respect for Nature and Property:** The Fenn treasure hunt reminded us that, while the thrill of the chase is enticing, it's important to respect the environment and follow ethical guidelines. Treasure hunting should not come at the expense of nature or the safety of others. In the case of the Fenn hunt, several searchers were injured or even lost their lives, highlighting the importance of safety, preparation, and ethical considerations in the pursuit of treasure.

- **Leave No Trace:** The Fenn hunt teaches us the value of "leave no trace" practices when exploring natural environments. This principle encourages treasure hunters to be responsible stewards of the land, ensuring that their activities do not damage the landscape, disrupt wildlife, or leave behind litter.

6. The Joy of the Hunt, Not Just the Treasure

Perhaps one of the most profound lessons from the Fenn treasure hunt is the idea that the treasure itself was not the true prize. For many participants, the joy came from the journey itself—solving riddles, exploring new places, and experiencing the thrill of discovery. While the final treasure was certainly valuable, the process of seeking it out brought participants closer to nature, enriched their lives, and allowed them to connect with like-minded adventurers.

- **The Treasure Is in the Journey:** Many hunters found personal satisfaction not in the discovery of the chest but in the experiences they gained along the way. Whether it was connecting with nature, overcoming obstacles, or learning new skills, the journey itself provided rewards that were as meaningful as any material wealth.

- **Personal Growth Through Adventure:** The Fenn hunt demonstrated how treasure hunting can be an avenue for personal growth. For many seekers, the hunt provided valuable lessons in perseverance, problem-solving, and resilience. The experience itself shaped who they were, offering opportunities for self-discovery that extended far beyond the treasure itself.

The Forrest Fenn treasure hunt, which captivated the imagination of thousands of people for nearly a decade, offered us important lessons in perseverance, collaboration, ethical exploration, and the joy of discovery. It reminded us that the true rewards of treasure hunting are often found not in the riches at the end of the journey but in the experiences, challenges, and personal growth gained along the way. Whether you're embarking on a similar adventure or simply reflecting on the lessons of Fenn's hunt, the key takeaway is clear: treasure hunting is about more than finding treasure. It's about the journey, the community, and the lessons learned in pursuit of the ultimate discovery.

Mindset for Treasure Hunting

Patience, Problem-Solving, and Perseverance

In any great treasure hunt, whether it involves physical riches or intellectual discovery, there are essential qualities that determine success or failure. Three of the most critical traits for any treasure seeker are patience, problem-solving, and perseverance. These characteristics aren't just helpful—they're necessary for navigating the complexities and challenges of the hunt. The journey is rarely straightforward, and the obstacles often require mental agility, adaptability, and the ability to stay focused on the ultimate goal despite setbacks. These qualities, when combined, form the foundation of successful treasure hunting and adventure.

1. Patience: The Art of Waiting and Reflecting

Patience is perhaps the most underrated trait when it comes to treasure hunting. A treasure hunt is rarely a race; instead, it's a slow and deliberate process that demands careful thought, observation, and reflection. Whether you're searching for buried treasure, solving riddles, or piecing together clues, each step requires a level of patience that allows you to process information, make connections, and avoid hasty decisions.

- **Avoiding Impulsive Decisions:** Many treasure hunters, especially those who are new to the game, may rush into the search, eager to find answers quickly. However, without patience, one may miss crucial clues or misinterpret important details. In the case of Forrest Fenn's treasure hunt, for example, countless hunters rushed to places based on hunches or overzealous interpretations of the clues, often overlooking subtle hints that might have steered them in the right direction. Patience gives you the space to thoroughly consider each element of the hunt before making decisions.

- **Allowing Time for Reflection:** Sometimes, stepping away from a problem or clue for a little while can offer fresh insights. Patience means giving yourself time to process and reflect, as it's easy to become too focused on one aspect of the hunt and miss the broader picture. This is particularly true for complex puzzles and riddles where new revelations often come when you least expect them. The ability to put down the map or riddle, take a break, and return with a clear mind can help you see things in a different light.

- **Taking in the Experience:** In a world that often values speed and efficiency, the act of patiently following a treasure hunt allows you to enjoy the journey itself. Many treasure seekers have spoken of the joy of exploration—whether it's hiking through unfamiliar terrain or researching historical artifacts—and how patience allows you to savor those moments. The quest for treasure is as much about personal growth and discovery as it is about finding a physical prize.

2. Problem-Solving: Decoding Clues and Unraveling Mysteries

Treasure hunts are essentially complex problems that need to be solved. Whether you're deciphering cryptic riddles, reading ancient maps, or interpreting obscure clues, the ability to problem-solve is central to your success. The process of breaking down the problem into smaller, more manageable parts, testing hypotheses, and revising strategies is what defines a successful treasure hunter.

- **Analyzing Clues Carefully:** One of the main aspects of problem-solving in a treasure hunt is the ability to analyze clues critically. The clues may not always be clear, and they may require you to think laterally—often, the answer is not what it first appears to be. In past treasure hunts, hunters have frequently found that solutions to riddles or clues were hidden within the very language of the puzzle itself, requiring a keen understanding of wordplay, symbols, or historical context. Problem-solving involves both recognizing patterns in the clues and making educated guesses when something isn't immediately obvious.

- **Testing Theories:** As you solve clues, you'll likely come up with multiple hypotheses or theories about where the treasure is hidden or how the riddle should be interpreted. A strong problem solver tests these theories against the clues to see if they hold up under scrutiny. Some treasure hunters may make mistakes or find themselves down the wrong path, but good problem-solvers are not afraid to revisit their theories and adjust their approach based on new evidence.

- **Breaking Down Complex Problems:** Some treasure hunts involve a series of interconnected clues that build on one another, requiring you to break down a larger problem into smaller, more digestible pieces. This process might involve working backward from a final goal or solving a series of smaller puzzles that gradually reveal the larger picture. Treasure hunts like the Forrest Fenn hunt, for example, included clues that involved both historical research and physical exploration, forcing hunters to apply various forms of problem-solving and integrate different types of knowledge.

3. Perseverance: Staying the Course Against All Odds

The final element that defines successful treasure hunting is perseverance—the ability to keep going despite challenges, setbacks, and obstacles. Whether it's dealing with physical exhaustion, interpreting a particularly difficult clue, or coping with moments of doubt, perseverance is what allows a hunter to continue their journey when it seems impossible.

- **Staying Motivated:** The road to discovering treasure is rarely a straight line. Along the way, you will encounter roadblocks, frustrations, and moments of failure. It is in these moments that perseverance becomes critical. Perseverance means staying focused on the goal, even when things aren't going well. A successful treasure hunter doesn't give up just because things are difficult; they push through obstacles, adapt to changing conditions, and remain determined to finish the quest.

- **Endurance Through Disappointment:** There will undoubtedly be moments of disappointment. Many treasure seekers in past hunts, including those looking for Fenn's treasure, experienced times when they felt like they were on the verge of success, only to have their hopes dashed. However, perseverance means that even after setbacks, the hunter returns to the search with renewed energy and determination. Each failure is an opportunity to learn, refine one's approach, and continue the journey.

- **Long-Term Commitment:** Treasure hunts, especially those that involve extensive searches in remote locations or solving intricate riddles, can take years. The Forrest Fenn treasure, for example, required participants to search vast stretches of rugged terrain, often enduring long periods of time without finding any tangible results. Perseverance allows you to remain committed to the hunt for the long haul, despite the challenges and uncertainties that may arise. This long-term focus, combined with patience, will ultimately lead to success.

- **Resilience and Adaptability:** Perseverance isn't just about stubbornly pursuing the same goal despite failure; it's about learning from experiences and adapting. As you encounter problems or new information, perseverance means adjusting your approach and continuing the hunt. Whether it's changing your search strategy, reanalyzing clues, or revisiting areas that you've already searched, perseverance requires flexibility and resilience in the face of adversity.

The Synergy Between Patience, Problem-Solving, and Perseverance

The true power of these three traits lies in how they complement each other. While patience allows you to take your time and avoid rushing, problem-solving gives you the tools to decode clues and approach challenges effectively. Perseverance ensures that you stay on track, even when the road gets tough, and keep trying until you reach your goal.

Together, patience, problem-solving, and perseverance form a powerful toolkit for any treasure hunter. When combined, these qualities not only improve your chances of success but also enrich your journey. Treasure hunting is as much about the process as it is about the reward, and by embodying these traits, you'll find that each challenge along the way becomes an opportunity to learn, grow, and ultimately succeed.

In the world of treasure hunting, few things are more essential than patience, problem-solving, and perseverance. These traits help navigate the unknown, turn obstacles into opportunities, and ensure that the journey, no matter how long or challenging, leads to success. Treasure hunts aren't won by those who rush or become discouraged but by those who remain steady, solve problems with creativity, and push forward even when faced with setbacks. As you embark on your own treasure hunt, remember these timeless lessons, for they are the key to unlocking both the riches and the deeper rewards that lie hidden along the way.

Balancing Fun with Focus

Treasure hunting is an exhilarating blend of adventure, discovery, and problem-solving, but it requires striking the right balance between enjoyment and determination. While the thrill of the journey and the excitement of exploring the unknown are vital to the experience, maintaining focus on the ultimate goal is equally important. Finding this equilibrium ensures that the process remains engaging without losing its purpose, allowing treasure hunters to fully embrace the journey while staying on course.

1. The Joy of the Hunt: Why Fun Matters

Treasure hunting inherently evokes a sense of play, curiosity, and wonder. It's an opportunity to step out of the routine and immerse oneself in an extraordinary adventure. However, the value of fun goes beyond mere enjoyment; it's a critical aspect of maintaining enthusiasm and energy throughout the journey.

- **Staying Motivated:** Treasure hunts can be lengthy and challenging, often requiring participants to spend hours, days, or even years deciphering clues and searching for hidden treasures. Infusing fun into the process keeps morale high and prevents burnout. Whether it's exploring breathtaking landscapes, uncovering historical tidbits, or sharing stories with fellow adventurers, the fun elements of the hunt make the effort feel worthwhile, even before the treasure is found.

- **Creative Thinking Through Play:** Relaxing and having fun can actually boost creativity. When treasure hunters approach the task with a sense of playfulness, they're more likely to think outside the box and come up with innovative solutions to complex problems. A lighthearted attitude often unlocks the kind of imaginative thinking needed to interpret cryptic clues or connect seemingly unrelated pieces of information.

- **Sharing the Adventure:** Treasure hunting is often a communal activity, whether you're working with a team or connecting with fellow hunters through shared experiences. Enjoying the process together strengthens bonds and builds camaraderie. Laughter, shared stories, and lighthearted moments can turn a challenging search into a lifelong memory.

2. The Need for Focus: Keeping Your Eyes on the Prize

While fun is essential, treasure hunting is ultimately a goal-oriented activity that requires concentration and discipline. Maintaining focus ensures that time, energy, and resources are directed toward solving the puzzles and reaching the final objective.

- **Avoiding Distractions:** The excitement of the hunt can sometimes lead to distractions. Beautiful landscapes, intriguing detours, or even overthinking small details can sidetrack treasure hunters from their main goal. Focus involves setting clear priorities and knowing when to move past tempting diversions that don't contribute to the hunt's success.

- **Developing a Clear Plan:** Staying focused often begins with a well-thought-out strategy. Treasure hunters benefit from mapping out their approach, breaking down tasks, and tackling each step methodically. A clear plan serves as a guide, preventing unnecessary wandering or getting lost in unproductive areas. It also helps maintain a sense of direction when faced with the inevitable frustrations or setbacks.

- **Overcoming Challenges:** Treasure hunting is rarely straightforward, and challenges such as deciphering cryptic clues or navigating difficult terrain require undivided attention. Staying focused allows hunters to channel their energy into problem-solving, ensuring they can analyze clues critically and persist through obstacles with determination.

3. Finding the Balance: Fun and Focus Working Together

Balancing fun with focus doesn't mean compartmentalizing these elements into separate moments; instead, it involves weaving them together seamlessly. The most successful treasure hunters know how to enjoy the process while remaining committed to their goals.

- **Staying Present in the Moment:** Balancing fun and focus begins with mindfulness—being present and engaged with the task at hand. When solving a puzzle, give it your full attention; when pausing to enjoy a beautiful view or share a laugh with friends, fully embrace the moment. Shifting between these modes with intention allows you to stay productive while still enjoying the journey.

- **Setting Milestones:** Breaking the hunt into smaller, achievable goals can help maintain both focus and fun. Celebrating small wins along the way—whether it's successfully solving a clue, reaching a landmark, or uncovering a fascinating piece of history—keeps spirits high and provides motivation to keep going.

- **Adopting a Flexible Mindset:** The unexpected is part of the adventure. Being open to surprises while staying committed to the goal allows for spontaneity without losing focus. For example, if a clue leads to an unexpectedly beautiful location, take time to appreciate it—but don't forget to revisit the clue with fresh eyes and continue the search.

- **Pacing Yourself:** Treasure hunting is often a marathon, not a sprint. Balancing fun and focus involves pacing yourself so that you have the energy and clarity needed to persist through long and challenging hunts. Allowing time for breaks, relaxation, and enjoyment ensures that you don't burn out while maintaining the focus needed to succeed.

4. The Deeper Rewards of Balance

Achieving a balance between fun and focus doesn't just enhance the treasure hunting experience—it also leads to deeper personal rewards. Treasure hunts are more than a quest for material riches; they are journeys of self-discovery, learning, and growth.

- **Cultivating Resilience:** Balancing fun with focus teaches valuable life skills, such as adaptability, patience, and perseverance. By navigating the ups and downs of the hunt with both joy and determination, treasure hunters develop resilience that carries over into other aspects of life.

- **Experiencing Joy Through Achievement:** Success feels even more rewarding when it's achieved through a process that was genuinely enjoyable. Balancing fun and focus ensures that the journey is as fulfilling as the destination, making the discovery of the treasure a triumphant culmination of both hard work and meaningful experiences.

- **Building Lifelong Memories:** The stories, laughs, and moments of awe experienced during a treasure hunt often linger long after the treasure itself is found. By embracing both fun and focus, participants create memories that become treasures in their own right—relics of an adventure that enriched their lives in unexpected ways.

Balancing fun with focus is the key to a fulfilling and successful treasure hunt. While the thrill of discovery and the joy of exploration keep the experience lighthearted and enjoyable, maintaining a clear focus ensures that the ultimate goal remains in sight. Together, these elements create a harmonious journey, where every clue solved and every step taken is imbued with meaning and joy. By embracing this balance, treasure hunters not only increase their chances of success but also enrich their journey with unforgettable moments and lasting rewards.

Global History and the Treasures of Life

Stories of Riches Across the Ages

Throughout history, tales of hidden wealth and treasure have captivated the human imagination, inspiring countless expeditions, legends, and cultural narratives. These stories, whether steeped in fact or spun from folklore, reveal humanity's enduring fascination with the idea of untold riches lying in wait for those brave or clever enough to find them. Each tale is more than just an account of gold and jewels—it is a reflection of the values, ambitions, and mysteries of its time. Here, we explore some of the most compelling stories of riches across the ages and their lasting significance.

1. Ancient Myths of Treasure

In the earliest civilizations, treasure often took on a mythical quality, representing divine favor, the bounty of nature, or the spoils of conquest.

- **King Midas and the Golden Touch:** In Greek mythology, King Midas was granted the power to turn everything he touched into gold. While his story serves as a cautionary tale about greed and excess, it also highlights how gold has long been a symbol of wealth and desire. Midas's tale underscores the human tendency to equate material wealth with happiness, even as it warns of the dangers of valuing riches above all else.

- **The Treasure of El Dorado:** The legend of El Dorado—a mythical city of gold—has lured explorers for centuries. Originating from tales told by indigenous peoples of South America, El Dorado symbolized untold riches waiting to be uncovered. Although no such city has ever been found, the quest for El Dorado spurred countless expeditions into uncharted territories, blending myth with the spirit of exploration.

- **Norse Legends of Hoarded Gold:** In Norse mythology, tales of buried treasure abound, often guarded by dragons or cursed by gods. The saga of Fafnir, a dwarf turned dragon to protect his hoard of gold, reflects the Norse view of wealth as both a source of power and a potential curse. Such tales reveal an enduring tension between the allure of treasure and the moral or spiritual costs of obtaining it.

2. Historical Treasures of Empires

As civilizations expanded and empires rose, treasure took on new forms, often tied to conquest, trade, and the accumulation of power.

- **The Lost Treasure of the Knights Templar:** The Knights Templar, a medieval Christian military order, were said to have amassed an immense fortune through their banking operations and control of trade routes. When the order was disbanded in the 14th century, rumors spread that their treasure was hidden away, fueling centuries of speculation and searches. From gold and jewels to religious relics like the Holy Grail, the Templar treasure remains one of history's most enduring mysteries.

- **The Aztec Gold of Montezuma:** When Hernán Cortés and his Spanish conquistadors arrived in the Aztec Empire in the early 16th century, they were dazzled by the wealth of Emperor Montezuma II. After the fall of the Aztec capital, legends arose of vast amounts of gold hidden by the Aztecs to keep it out of Spanish hands. Known as "Montezuma's Treasure," this gold has never been found, sparking theories about its fate and fueling expeditions in Mexico.

- **The Wealth of Ancient Egypt:** The pharaohs of ancient Egypt were renowned for their elaborate burial practices, which included entombing their dead with vast treasures. The discovery of King Tutankhamun's tomb in 1922 revealed a trove of gold artifacts, jewelry, and other riches that had remained untouched for over 3,000 years. These treasures not only showcased the opulence of ancient Egyptian culture but also provided invaluable insights into their beliefs about the afterlife.

3. Maritime Treasures of the Golden Age of Piracy

The oceans have long been a repository for untold riches, from shipwrecks laden with gold to legendary pirate hoards.

- **The Spanish Galleons and the Treasure Fleets:** In the 16th and 17th centuries, Spain transported immense quantities of gold and silver from the Americas to Europe via treasure fleets. Many of these ships were lost to storms, shipwrecks, or pirate attacks, leaving vast amounts of wealth lying on the ocean floor.

Modern-day salvage operations have recovered portions of this treasure, but much remains undiscovered.

- **The Infamous Pirate Captain Kidd:** One of the most famous stories of buried treasure is tied to Captain William Kidd, a Scottish pirate of the late 17th century. Before his capture and execution, Kidd allegedly buried a treasure trove of gold, silver, and jewels on Gardiners Island off the coast of New York. Though parts of his treasure have been recovered, much of it remains the subject of speculation and intrigue.

- **The Treasure of the Whydah Gally:** In 1717, the pirate ship Whydah Gally sank off the coast of Cape Cod, Massachusetts, carrying a hoard of loot from over 50 captured ships. In the 1980s, modern treasure hunters discovered the wreck and began recovering gold coins, silver ingots, and artifacts, proving that the legends of pirate treasure are more than just tall tales.

4. Modern-Day Tales of Treasure

Even in recent history, the allure of hidden riches has continued to inspire treasure hunts and discoveries.

- **The Forrest Fenn Treasure:** In 2010, millionaire art dealer Forrest Fenn hid a chest filled with gold, rare coins, and gemstones somewhere in the Rocky Mountains and published a cryptic poem containing clues to its location. The treasure sparked a decade-long hunt that attracted thousands of searchers, culminating in its discovery in 2020. Fenn's treasure is a modern example of how the ancient thrill of the hunt still resonates today.

- **The Oak Island Mystery:** Off the coast of Nova Scotia, Canada, lies Oak Island, a site famous for its supposed buried treasure. For over 200 years, treasure hunters have sought to uncover the contents of the island's "Money Pit," believed to contain pirate gold, historical artifacts, or even religious relics. Despite extensive excavations and numerous theories, the mystery remains unsolved.

5. The Cultural Significance of Treasure Stories

Beyond their entertainment value, stories of riches across the ages offer insights into human nature, societal values, and cultural history.

- **Symbolism of Wealth:** In many stories, treasure represents more than material wealth—it embodies power, freedom, or the fulfillment of dreams. Whether it's the promise of a better life, the allure of adventure, or the thrill of solving a mystery, treasure serves as a metaphor for human aspiration.

- **Moral Lessons:** Many treasure stories include cautionary elements, warning of the dangers of greed or the corrupting influence of wealth. From King Midas's golden touch to the cursed Aztec gold of pirate lore, these tales remind us that the pursuit of riches can come with unintended consequences.

- **Inspiring Exploration:** Tales of treasure have historically motivated exploration and discovery. The search for riches drove European explorers to the New World, adventurers to remote jungles and deserts, and modern treasure hunters to push the boundaries of technology and innovation.

The stories of riches across the ages are more than just thrilling tales; they are a reflection of humanity's enduring relationship with wealth, mystery, and adventure. From ancient myths and royal treasures to pirate hoards and modern hunts, these narratives captivate the imagination and inspire both awe and curiosity. Whether rooted in fact or born of legend, they remind us of the timeless allure of the unknown and the universal desire to uncover something extraordinary hidden just beneath the surface.

Personal Development Through the Search

Embarking on a treasure hunt is about far more than discovering physical riches; it is a journey of personal growth and self-discovery. The process of searching for treasure inherently challenges individuals to develop resilience, sharpen their minds, and deepen their understanding of themselves and the world around them. Treasure hunts are not only about solving riddles or traversing uncharted terrain but also about embracing the opportunities they provide for personal development along the way.

1. Cultivating Resilience and Perseverance

Treasure hunting often requires patience and the ability to face and overcome obstacles. From deciphering complex clues to dealing with physical and environmental challenges, hunters are frequently tested, learning to persevere even when the odds seem insurmountable.

- **Learning to Embrace Setbacks:** The path to treasure is rarely straightforward. Dead ends, misinterpretations, and missed opportunities are part of the process. These moments teach hunters to see setbacks as stepping stones rather than failures, cultivating resilience that extends beyond the hunt.

- **Building Mental Stamina:** Treasure hunting demands sustained effort over time. Developing the discipline to keep pushing forward, even when progress is slow, strengthens mental fortitude, a quality that is valuable in all aspects of life.

2. Enhancing Problem-Solving Skills

At the heart of every treasure hunt is a series of puzzles, riddles, and mysteries waiting to be unraveled. Engaging with these challenges sharpens cognitive abilities and encourages innovative thinking.

- **Critical Thinking:** Clues often require logical reasoning and the ability to analyze information from different perspectives. Treasure hunters learn to break problems into manageable parts, evaluate possible solutions, and select the most plausible course of action.

- **Creative Problem-Solving:** Many riddles in treasure hunts defy conventional thinking, requiring hunters to think outside the box. This practice of creative problem-solving fosters adaptability and resourcefulness—skills that are invaluable in everyday life.

- **Collaboration and Communication:** When treasure hunting in teams, participants must work together to pool knowledge, share insights, and coordinate efforts. Effective communication and collaboration are essential, helping to refine social and leadership skills.

3. Connecting with the Natural and Historical World

Treasure hunts often lead participants to explore diverse environments and learn about the history of the places they visit. This exposure fosters a deeper appreciation for the world and its rich tapestry of stories.

- **Discovering Hidden Landscapes:** Whether searching through dense forests, vast deserts, or coastal shores, hunters often find themselves in awe-inspiring settings. These experiences deepen their connection to nature and inspire a sense of wonder and respect for the planet.

- **Exploring Historical Narratives:** Many treasure hunts are rooted in historical events, legends, or artifacts. Engaging with these stories broadens participants' understanding of different cultures and time periods, enriching their worldview and sparking curiosity about the past.

4. Cultivating Emotional Growth

The emotional journey of a treasure hunt can be as transformative as the physical and intellectual aspects. Hunters often confront their fears, test their limits, and discover inner strengths they didn't know they possessed.

- **Managing Uncertainty and Risk:** Treasure hunting involves stepping into the unknown, embracing uncertainty, and taking calculated risks. This experience builds confidence and reduces the fear of failure, encouraging a more adventurous approach to life.

- **Experiencing the Joy of Discovery:** The thrill of solving a difficult riddle, reaching a key milestone, or simply uncovering a piece of history fosters a profound sense of accomplishment. These moments of joy and triumph boost self-esteem and provide lasting motivation.

- **Fostering Gratitude and Reflection:** The journey itself often becomes a source of gratitude. Whether it's appreciating the beauty of the landscapes explored, the camaraderie of fellow adventurers, or the lessons learned along the way, hunters frequently find themselves reflecting on the value of the experience beyond the material prize.

5. Unlocking a Growth Mindset

A growth mindset—the belief that abilities and intelligence can be developed through effort and learning—is an essential part of treasure hunting. The challenges and triumphs encountered on the hunt encourage individuals to embrace learning opportunities and push past self-imposed limits.

- **Learning from Mistakes:** Treasure hunters often learn that mistakes are not failures but opportunities to refine their strategies and improve. This mindset fosters resilience and encourages lifelong learning.

- **Developing Patience and Persistence:** The complexity of treasure hunts demands patience and persistence. Hunters quickly realize that progress often comes in small increments and that dedication to the process is as important as the outcome.

- **Embracing the Journey:** A growth mindset shifts the focus from the end goal to the journey itself. Treasure hunters learn to value the experiences, relationships, and personal growth that occur along the way, making the search as rewarding as the discovery.

6. Gaining Lifelong Skills

The skills honed during a treasure hunt are not confined to the search itself; they translate into real-world advantages that enrich many aspects of life.

- **Enhanced Attention to Detail:** Deciphering clues and searching for hidden treasures sharpens observational skills and attention to detail, abilities that prove useful in professional and personal contexts alike.

- **Improved Decision-Making:** Navigating a treasure hunt requires quick thinking and sound judgment, skills that are transferable to work, relationships, and daily problem-solving.

- **Time and Resource Management:** Effective treasure hunters learn to allocate their time, energy, and tools wisely, balancing exploration with strategy. These lessons in resourcefulness and planning carry over into life's challenges.

7. Transformative Insights

Perhaps the most profound aspect of personal development through treasure hunting is the transformation it brings. By pushing boundaries, embracing uncertainty, and celebrating victories, treasure hunters emerge from the experience with a deeper understanding of themselves and a greater appreciation for life's adventures.

- **A Sense of Accomplishment:** Completing a treasure hunt, or even making significant progress, provides a powerful sense of achievement that reinforces self-belief and resilience.

- **Discovery of New Passions:** The process often leads to the discovery of unexpected interests, whether it's a love for history, a fascination with puzzles, or a newfound appreciation for nature.

- **The Joy of Lifelong Learning:** Treasure hunting instills a curiosity and love for exploration that lasts long after the hunt is over, encouraging participants to seek out new challenges and adventures.

Personal development through treasure hunting is a profound and multifaceted journey. The search for physical riches mirrors an inner quest for growth, pushing participants to develop resilience, problem-solving skills, and emotional strength. Along the way, they gain a deeper connection to history, nature, and their own potential. While the ultimate treasure may be the goal, the transformative experiences and lessons learned along the way are the true rewards, shaping individuals into more confident, capable, and fulfilled adventurers.

The Joy of Discovery

Celebrating Small Wins Along the Way

The journey of treasure hunting, like any grand adventure, is not defined solely by the final discovery of riches or the achievement of the ultimate goal. Rather, it is the accumulation of small wins—those moments of progress, insight, and minor successes—that truly shape the experience. Celebrating these small victories along the way is not just a way to stay motivated, but also a reminder of the value inherent in the process itself. These moments of accomplishment, whether big or small, are integral to sustaining enthusiasm, building momentum, and fostering a sense of fulfillment.

1. Recognizing Progress

In any long-term pursuit, especially one as intricate and challenging as a treasure hunt, it's easy to become fixated on the end goal. However, focusing only on the final prize can lead to frustration, impatience, and burnout. Celebrating small wins helps to shift the focus to the journey itself, encouraging treasure hunters to take pride in the steps they've taken and the progress they've made.

- **Breaking Down the Journey:** A treasure hunt often involves a series of steps, whether it's solving a difficult riddle, reaching a new location, or discovering a previously overlooked clue. By recognizing these smaller victories, hunters can take satisfaction in their progress and see how each achievement contributes to the larger goal.

- **Tracking Milestones:** One effective way to celebrate small wins is by marking specific milestones along the way. Perhaps it's cracking a particularly challenging puzzle, uncovering a historical detail, or narrowing down the search area. These moments can be documented and celebrated, reminding participants of their growth and the skills they've developed throughout the process.

2. Boosting Motivation

Treasure hunting can be a long and demanding process, and it's easy to feel discouraged when the goal seems distant. Acknowledging and celebrating the small wins offers a powerful antidote to the frustration that may arise during the search.

These small successes provide a sense of accomplishment and pride, fueling the drive to continue pushing forward.

- **Psychological Benefits:** Celebrating small wins releases dopamine, a neurotransmitter associated with feelings of pleasure and accomplishment. This chemical boost can significantly improve mood and motivation, helping participants maintain a positive mindset and reinforcing the desire to keep going, even in the face of setbacks.

- **Reaffirming the Goal:** Every small win serves as a reminder of the larger goal, reinforcing the purpose of the treasure hunt and the reason for embarking on this journey in the first place. Whether it's the joy of solving a complex riddle or uncovering a hidden landmark, these moments help to maintain clarity and focus on the ultimate objective.

3. Cultivating a Sense of Gratitude

Treasure hunts often involve exploration of unfamiliar places, the discovery of rare items, and encounters with new perspectives. By taking time to appreciate the small victories along the way, treasure hunters can develop a deeper sense of gratitude for the journey itself. This appreciation can enhance the overall experience and promote a positive, open-minded attitude.

- **Appreciating the Process:** Celebrating small wins encourages participants to savor the journey rather than rushing toward the finish line. Each clue, each step forward, and each challenge overcome is an opportunity to reflect on the experiences gained and the lessons learned.

- **Acknowledging the Beauty in the Journey:** Whether it's the beauty of the natural landscape, the thrill of a new discovery, or the joy of shared experiences with fellow adventurers, small wins help to highlight the wonders of the journey that might otherwise be overlooked.

4. Strengthening Confidence

Every small victory in a treasure hunt builds confidence, providing a sense of competence and capability. As participants successfully solve clues, navigate difficult terrain, or make breakthroughs in their research, they gain a greater belief in their abilities. These small successes serve as evidence of progress, reinforcing the idea that the ultimate goal is achievable.

- **Building Momentum:** Each small win creates momentum, making the next challenge feel more manageable and achievable. As hunters accumulate successes, their confidence grows, enabling them to take on increasingly difficult tasks with a sense of assurance and competence.

- **Overcoming Self-Doubt:** Treasure hunting, especially when facing difficult challenges, can sometimes trigger self-doubt. Celebrating small wins serves as a reminder that progress is being made, even when the path forward isn't immediately clear. These moments of success help to counterbalance feelings of uncertainty and build the mental resilience needed to stay the course.

5. Creating a Positive and Supportive Environment

In some treasure hunts, participants may be working as part of a team, or they may be sharing their journey with others—whether through social media, blogs, or in-person interactions. Celebrating small wins is an excellent way to create a positive atmosphere and inspire others to engage in the journey.

- **Team Morale:** In group treasure hunts, recognizing and celebrating small successes together strengthens team morale. Whether it's an encouraging word, a shared moment of triumph, or a celebratory gesture, these small victories help to keep the team motivated and cohesive.

- **Encouraging Others:** Celebrating your own small wins can inspire others who may be engaged in the same hunt or have embarked on their own quests. When individuals see others celebrate progress, it can create a ripple effect that encourages them to keep going, even when they encounter obstacles.

- **Fostering a Spirit of Camaraderie:** The shared joy of celebrating small wins fosters a sense of camaraderie and connection. In group hunts, this can be especially important, as the bonds created during moments of success contribute to a collective sense of achievement.

6. Reaffirming the Purpose

Celebrating small wins serves as a powerful reminder of the original purpose behind the treasure hunt. Whether it's a search for adventure, personal growth, historical discovery, or even charity, these moments of success offer the opportunity to reconnect with the values and motivations that drove participants to begin the hunt in the first place.

- **Reflecting on the Bigger Picture:** While individual clues and steps may seem insignificant in the grand scheme, celebrating small wins helps to highlight how each moment fits into the broader narrative. These reflections can reignite the passion and excitement that initially sparked the search.

- **Embracing the Adventure:** Ultimately, the small victories in a treasure hunt help participants embrace the adventure itself, reminding them that the experience is just as important—if not more so—than the destination. By celebrating progress, participants cultivate an attitude of gratitude and mindfulness that enhances every part of the journey.

7. Practicing Joy in the Moment

Life is full of larger goals and ultimate ambitions, but it's the moments along the way that often bring the most joy. Celebrating small wins allows treasure hunters to practice being present, to enjoy each victory as it comes, and to acknowledge the happiness found in the search itself.

- **Living in the Present:** Celebrating small wins encourages participants to stay present and mindful, savoring the moment rather than rushing toward the next milestone. These moments of joy and celebration deepen the overall experience, allowing hunters to derive more pleasure from the process, rather than solely from the outcome.

- **Finding Meaning in Every Step:** Every clue solved, every puzzle cracked, and every challenge overcome adds meaning to the adventure. By celebrating these small wins, hunters acknowledge the richness of the journey and the sense of fulfillment that comes from each step forward.

Treasure hunting is more than just a pursuit of hidden riches—it is a journey that unfolds with each small win. Celebrating these moments of progress is essential not only for maintaining motivation but also for enriching the overall experience. By recognizing the significance of each success, treasure hunters can stay energized, strengthen their confidence, and cultivate a sense of gratitude for the process itself. These small wins create lasting memories, forge deeper connections with the journey, and remind participants that the adventure is as valuable as the treasure at the end of the hunt.

Connecting With the Stories Behind the Treasures

A treasure hunt is not simply about finding material wealth or rare items—it's about uncovering the rich, often hidden stories behind the treasures themselves. Every artifact, gem, or piece of historical memorabilia carries with it a tale that transcends its value or appearance. These stories, whether they stem from history, art, culture, or personal journeys, are as significant as the treasures themselves. By connecting with these stories, treasure hunters gain a deeper understanding of the world around them and a more meaningful connection to the items they uncover. The narrative behind each treasure breathes life into the hunt and provides a broader context for its importance.

1. The Power of Storytelling in Treasure Hunts

At the heart of any treasure hunt lies storytelling. The items being sought after often have fascinating histories—stories of their creation, the people who owned them, the places they've been, and the circumstances under which they were hidden or lost. These stories offer more than just an intellectual connection; they engage the emotions, ignite curiosity, and spark an appreciation for the significance of the treasure.

- **Emotional Connection:** When we hear a compelling story behind an item— whether it's a priceless gem once owned by royalty, a Picasso painting that changed the course of art, or a rare artifact with a powerful historical narrative—we develop an emotional connection to it. It's no longer just a material object but a piece of history, a symbol of human achievement, and a link to the past.

- **Fostering a Sense of Wonder:** The stories behind treasures often come with a sense of mystery and intrigue. Was the treasure hidden on purpose? Who was the original owner? What did it represent to those who sought it, or those who fought for it? These stories captivate the imagination and invite treasure hunters to reflect on the layers of meaning that lie beneath the surface.

2. Understanding the History and Significance of Treasures

One of the most profound aspects of a treasure hunt is the opportunity to delve into the historical significance of the treasures being sought. Whether the items are ancient relics, precious gemstones, or pieces of modern art, each treasure carries a unique historical context. Connecting with the stories behind the treasures allows hunters to better understand their cultural, political, and social importance.

- **Cultural and Historical Context:** Treasures often have a connection to a specific culture, period, or historical event. For example, an antique piece of jewelry may offer insight into the craftsmanship and fashion of an era long past, while a rare coin could provide a glimpse into the economy and values of a forgotten civilization. Understanding this context enriches the experience of searching for the treasure, as the item becomes a symbol of a larger story.

- **The Legacy of the Past:** Each treasure reflects a chapter in history, whether it was part of a family heirloom passed down through generations, a war relic from a forgotten conflict, or a piece of art that shaped cultural movements. Connecting with these stories allows treasure hunters to feel like part of the larger narrative of human progress, giving the search meaning that goes beyond the thrill of the hunt.

3. The Personal Journeys of Previous Owners

Many treasures are tied to the personal journeys of individuals who owned, cherished, or lost them. These stories—whether tragic, heroic, or even romantic—add depth to the treasure hunt and help hunters empathize with those who came before them. By learning about the lives of previous owners, treasure hunters are invited to connect with the human aspect of the treasure, further enhancing its value and significance.

- **The Stories of Past Seekers:** In some cases, treasures were hidden away or lost due to the actions of those who sought them, whether out of necessity, greed, or a desire for protection. The quest to recover such treasures may involve uncovering the motivations and actions of past treasure seekers, making the story of the treasure even richer.

- **Personal Connections to the Past:** When treasure hunters learn the personal history of an item, they can begin to understand why it mattered to its previous owners. Perhaps the item was a symbol of a great love, a token of success, or a symbol of sacrifice. These personal connections provide emotional depth and a deeper appreciation for the treasure, as it becomes not just an object, but a piece of someone's life and legacy.

4. The Adventure of Discovery

The hunt itself is often a journey of discovery—not only of physical treasures but also of the stories that surround them. Every clue uncovered, every mystery solved, opens a new chapter in the tale. For treasure hunters, learning about the history behind the treasure enhances the joy of the quest, as it turns the search into a deeper exploration of human history, art, and culture.

- **Unraveling the Mystery:** As clues lead treasure hunters closer to their prize, they may begin to piece together the story of the treasure. Was it hidden by an explorer? Stolen from an ancient tomb? Commissioned by a famous artist? These questions drive the hunt and keep participants invested in learning more about the treasure's origins. Each revelation adds to the excitement, not just because of the treasure itself, but because of the story being unraveled.

- **Living the Story:** When treasure hunters connect with the stories behind the treasures they are seeking, they begin to live out a part of the narrative. The search itself becomes an adventure filled with twists, turns, and discoveries, much like the tales of those who sought treasure in the past. This deeper involvement in the story creates a sense of belonging to a much larger historical adventure, where every new piece of information adds to the richness of the experience.

5. Drawing Parallels Between the Past and Present

Connecting with the stories behind treasures also encourages treasure hunters to draw parallels between the past and their own lives. The themes found in the tales of treasures—such as resilience, discovery, ambition, and the pursuit of greatness—are timeless and universal. By exploring these stories, hunters may find themselves inspired by the courage and determination of past adventurers, and perhaps even inspired to embark on their own personal quests for meaning.

- **Universal Themes:** The stories behind treasures often center on universal themes such as love, loss, conflict, and triumph. These themes resonate with treasure hunters on a deeply personal level, providing lessons and reflections that extend beyond the treasure hunt itself. Whether it's the pursuit of wealth, the desire to honor a legacy, or the quest for adventure, these timeless motifs create a bond between the past and present.

- **Personal Reflection:** As treasure hunters connect with the stories behind the treasures, they may find themselves reflecting on their own lives and motivations. What drives them to seek treasure? What personal journeys are they undertaking in parallel? These reflections not only deepen their connection to the hunt but also offer valuable insights into their own personal growth and desires.

6. Inspiring Future Generations

The stories behind treasures have the power to inspire not only those who are actively participating in the hunt but also future generations. By sharing these stories, treasure hunters contribute to a larger cultural narrative that enriches the collective understanding of human history, creativity, and adventure.

- **Preserving Stories for the Future:** The act of preserving and sharing the stories behind treasures ensures that they are passed down to future generations. As treasures are uncovered, their histories are brought to life, providing educational opportunities and fostering a deeper appreciation for the world's cultural heritage.

- **Passing the Torch:** When treasure hunters connect with the stories behind their finds, they are not just continuing a search—they are carrying forward a legacy. By sharing their discoveries and the stories that accompany them, they inspire others to seek knowledge, adventure, and personal growth.

Connecting with the stories behind treasures is what transforms a simple hunt into an enriching experience. These stories deepen the meaning of the treasures, offering treasure hunters not only the excitement of discovery but also the joy of learning about history, art, culture, and the people who lived before them. Each treasure has a tale to tell, and by connecting with these narratives, hunters can gain a fuller appreciation of the journey they are on, enrich their understanding of the world, and carry with them a legacy of exploration and discovery that extends far beyond the physical treasures they uncover.

The First Chest

Clues, Riddles, and Hidden Hints

At the core of any treasure hunt lies the intricate web of clues, riddles, and hidden hints that guide the seeker toward the prize. These elements are not just obstacles to be overcome but are the very fabric of the adventure itself, transforming the search into a puzzle that requires wit, creativity, and perseverance. They inject an element of mystery and challenge into the quest, and the ability to decipher these enigmatic messages is what separates the casual adventurer from the true treasure hunter. The beauty of a well-crafted clue or riddle is its dual nature: it is both a test and a reward, offering a glimpse of the treasure while pushing the seeker to think critically and embrace the thrill of discovery.

1. The Role of Clues in a Treasure Hunt

Clues are the foundation of a treasure hunt, providing the necessary direction and framework for the journey. A clue can be anything from a physical object to a coded message, a riddle, or even a subtle reference in a historical text. Clues often come in layers, each leading to the next, creating a sequence that challenges the hunter's perception and deductive reasoning. They are carefully designed to spark curiosity, deepen the mystery, and ultimately bring the hunter closer to the ultimate goal.

- **Guiding the Seeker:** A well-placed clue serves as a marker, pointing the hunter in the right direction. It could be an encoded message, a strange symbol, or even a reference to a historical event or location. Each clue gives the seeker a piece of the puzzle, encouraging them to dig deeper and unravel the mystery step by step.

- **Building Suspense and Excitement:** The thrill of uncovering a clue adds a layer of suspense to the treasure hunt. Each clue brings the hunter closer to solving the puzzle, but it also raises new questions and challenges. This process of constant discovery and revelation keeps the hunter engaged, driven by the desire to solve the next part of the riddle.

2. The Mystery and Power of Riddles

Riddles have been used throughout history as a clever and poetic way to pass on knowledge, challenge the intellect, and conceal information. In the context of a treasure hunt, riddles serve not only as clues but as intellectual challenges that require a unique combination of logic, creativity, and lateral thinking. Solving a riddle is often the moment of breakthrough in a treasure hunt—when the answer to a perplexing question opens the door to the next phase of the search.

- **Wordplay and Double Meanings:** A riddle's strength lies in its ability to obscure the answer through wordplay, double meanings, or ambiguous phrasing. For example, a riddle might use metaphors, allusions, or historical references that, at first glance, don't seem to relate to the treasure at all. This forces the hunter to think outside the box, exploring possible interpretations and alternative meanings.

- **Eliciting Intuition and Insight:** While riddles may seem like intellectual exercises, they also tap into the treasure hunter's intuition. Often, the best solutions come not from logical analysis alone but from an intuitive flash of insight, a "gut feeling" that guides the hunter toward the correct answer. This combination of reason and intuition makes riddles both frustrating and exhilarating to solve.

3. Hidden Hints and Subtle Details

Hidden hints are the most elusive of the three puzzle elements, often buried in plain sight or concealed within everyday objects, artworks, or locations. These hints may be disguised in cryptic symbols, subtle changes in the environment, or overlooked details in a map or text. To uncover these hidden hints, the treasure hunter must possess a sharp eye, a keen sense of observation, and a deep awareness of the surroundings.

- **The Art of Observation:** Hidden hints often lie in plain sight, tucked away in mundane objects or architectural details. A seemingly insignificant crack in a wall, a pattern in the surrounding landscape, or a faded inscription on a building might hold the key to advancing the hunt. The key to discovering these subtle clues is the ability to notice what others might overlook. Treasure hunters must constantly remain vigilant, seeing beyond the obvious to uncover these hidden treasures.

- **Interpreting the Environment:** Hidden hints can also be embedded in the environment itself. The way sunlight hits a particular spot at a specific time of day, the positioning of landmarks, or even the arrangement of natural features may provide critical clues. Understanding the interplay between clues and the physical environment can help the seeker uncover important hidden messages that would otherwise be missed.

4. The Challenge of Decoding

A significant part of treasure hunting involves the decoding of clues, riddles, and hints. This requires the hunter to not only solve puzzles but to understand the context, recognize patterns, and apply a variety of intellectual and practical skills. Decoding can involve knowledge of languages, history, geography, cryptography, and even art. The challenge comes from piecing together disparate fragments of information, each leading closer to the hidden prize.

- **Cryptography and Ciphers:** One common form of clue in a treasure hunt is the use of ciphers or codes, which require specialized knowledge to break. From simple substitution ciphers to more complex encryption techniques, decoding a message is an intellectual challenge that requires both analytical thinking and a familiarity with historical or contemporary methods of cryptography.

- **Historical References and Allusions:** Many clues are rooted in history, literature, or culture. The key to decoding these types of hints is having a broad knowledge base or knowing where to look. A riddle might reference a famous event, a well-known work of literature, or a significant cultural symbol, and recognizing these references can unlock the solution.

- **Puzzle Solving and Pattern Recognition:** Puzzle-solving is another critical skill for decoding clues and riddles. Many treasure hunts rely on the recognition of patterns, whether they are numerical, linguistic, or visual. The ability to discern these patterns and apply logical reasoning will help the seeker decode even the most cryptic messages.

5. The Joy of Discovery

Each time a clue is deciphered, a riddle is solved, or a hidden hint is uncovered, the treasure hunter experiences a small but profound victory. These moments of discovery, while often fleeting, are the heart of the treasure hunt. They offer not only a sense of progress but also a surge of excitement, as the next piece of the puzzle falls into place.

- **The Thrill of Unraveling Mysteries:** There is an innate thrill in solving a riddle or decoding a message. It's like solving a mini mystery within a larger story. Each small victory is a step toward a much larger achievement, and the satisfaction of discovering the meaning behind a clue propels the hunter forward in the quest.

- **Building Confidence:** Each solved clue boosts the hunter's confidence, reaffirming their ability to meet the challenges ahead. As the hunt progresses, the seeker becomes more adept at spotting patterns, analyzing details, and interpreting cryptic messages. These moments of success build momentum, making the next puzzle seem more manageable and achievable.

6. Clues, Riddles, and the Treasure Hunt Experience

Ultimately, the clues, riddles, and hidden hints are what make a treasure hunt truly magical. They transform the search from a mere pursuit of material wealth into an intellectual adventure that engages the mind and senses, creating a richer, more rewarding experience. The thrill of discovering hidden meanings, deciphering codes, and unraveling complex puzzles becomes as valuable as the treasure itself.

- **The Treasure Hunt as a Journey:** A successful treasure hunt is not just about the destination, but about the journey of discovery along the way. The process of solving clues and riddles brings a sense of accomplishment, intellectual satisfaction, and emotional fulfillment. It allows hunters to engage with the treasure hunt in a deeper way, transforming it into a personal and transformative journey.

- **Enduring Satisfaction:** Even after the final treasure is uncovered, the experience of solving the clues, deciphering the riddles, and connecting the hidden hints lingers. It becomes a story to tell, a puzzle solved, and a challenge met. The joy of discovery and the satisfaction of unraveling a complex mystery stay with the hunter long after the treasure has been claimed.

Clues, riddles, and hidden hints form the backbone of a treasure hunt, providing both the challenge and the joy of discovery. They guide the treasure hunter through an intellectual and emotional journey, transforming the search into a meaningful pursuit. By solving these puzzles and uncovering hidden messages, hunters engage not only with the quest itself but with history, culture, and the human experience. In the end, the true treasure lies not just in the riches found, but in the process of discovery, the thrill of the chase, and the satisfaction of connecting with the mysteries that lie hidden beneath the surface.

The Second Chest

Clues, Riddles, and Hidden Hints

The second chest is an integral milestone in the treasure hunt, an exciting continuation of the journey that both deepens the mystery and intensifies the challenge. After successfully navigating the first set of clues, the hunter now faces a more complex and engaging set of riddles, hidden hints, and challenging puzzles designed to refine their skills and push their thinking. The clues for this chest are meant to stretch the boundaries of logic and intuition, requiring the hunter to think creatively and remain flexible in their approach. Every clue, riddle, and hidden hint brings the seeker closer to the treasure, but also demands persistence, patience, and a keen eye.

1. The Challenge of the Second Chest

The second chest doesn't just build on the knowledge gained from the first but introduces a new layer of difficulty, demanding a more nuanced understanding of the hunt's overall structure. The clues may become more abstract, cryptic, or complex, requiring the hunter to combine knowledge from different fields—history, art, geography, and even cryptography. The riddles may reference more obscure facts, and the hidden hints may be harder to recognize, perhaps hidden in plain sight or embedded in seemingly unrelated objects or texts. This shift is intentional: it prepares the treasure hunter for even greater challenges ahead, testing both intellect and resourcefulness.

- **Increasing Complexity:** With the second chest, the treasure hunt introduces new methods for deciphering clues. Unlike the first chest, where answers might have been relatively straightforward, these clues require more critical thinking and often a multi-step process. This is where the treasure hunter learns to spot patterns, connect disparate pieces of information, and make intuitive leaps. It's a reminder that treasure hunting is not just about finding the right location but about seeing the story unfold as one progresses.

- **Riddles That Test Your Logic:** The riddles associated with the second chest are likely to require a more detailed interpretation. They might contain wordplay or ask the hunter to make connections between disparate ideas or historical facts. For example, a riddle could reference a specific place, an obscure historical event, or an abstract concept that forces the seeker to think beyond conventional boundaries. To solve these riddles, the treasure hunter must not only focus on the words but also on their underlying meaning, searching for the subtle connections that lead to the answer.

2. Hidden Hints: The Subtle Clues That Shape the Path

Hidden hints are the most elusive and delicate part of the second chest's puzzle. These hints are often concealed within the environment, objects, or artifacts connected to the chest. A hidden hint might not always be an obvious clue but rather a detail that requires careful observation and attention. The hunter must learn to read between the lines, understanding that sometimes what is most important is not what's immediately visible but the details that lie beneath the surface.

- **Environmental Clues:** Hidden hints often require the treasure hunter to pay close attention to their surroundings. The position of landmarks, the way shadows fall at specific times of day, the patterns on a map, or even subtle alterations in the environment could all contain crucial information. For instance, an inscription on a stone wall might seem unimportant at first, but upon further inspection, it could reveal a hidden symbol or clue that directs the hunter closer to the second chest.

- **Artifact and Object-Based Clues:** Many treasure hunts incorporate objects— pieces of art, historical artifacts, or everyday items—that contain hidden hints. These objects often have inscriptions, carvings, or subtle markers that lead the hunter to the next step. For example, a seemingly innocuous object like a vintage compass could have a hidden engraving that points to a specific direction or location. By studying these objects with fresh eyes, the treasure hunter uncovers the hidden meanings within.

- **Subtle Details in Texts and Symbols:** In many treasure hunts, texts or symbols can offer hidden hints. A poem or passage of historical writing, for instance, may contain hidden references to places, people, or events that the seeker must connect to the puzzle. Similarly, symbols—whether on maps, drawings, or in the architecture of the surroundings—can hold important information that leads to the next chest. These hints may seem innocuous at first glance, but with careful analysis, they can reveal critical pieces of the puzzle.

3. Decoding and Problem-Solving: The Key to Progress

Decoding the riddles, understanding the hidden hints, and connecting all the dots is where the treasure hunt truly begins to challenge the seeker's problem-solving abilities. Each clue is part of a larger narrative, and the hunter must assemble the pieces like a jigsaw puzzle, making connections that might not be immediately obvious. Solving the riddles often requires a combination of creative thinking, logic, and an understanding of history, geography, and other relevant knowledge. The more knowledge the hunter has about the world, the better equipped they will be to make sense of the clues.

- **Patience and Perseverance:** The key to cracking the riddle and unveiling the hidden hints lies in the ability to stay patient and persistent. The second chest's clues may not yield their secrets easily. The treasure hunter may need to revisit locations, reanalyze texts, or reframe riddles multiple times before the answer becomes clear. The act of problem-solving is as much about persistence as it is about intellect. At times, the most elusive clues only reveal themselves after hours of thoughtful analysis or after the hunter takes a step back and allows the subconscious to connect the dots.

- **Connecting the Dots:** A key component in solving the riddles and uncovering hidden hints is pattern recognition. The second chest, in particular, often requires the hunter to connect seemingly unrelated pieces of information. A small clue on a map might align with a line in a poem, which in turn might correspond to a historical figure or place. It's this intricate web of connections that makes the treasure hunt so captivating. Each small revelation feeds into the larger picture, leading to the chest.

4. The Satisfaction of Uncovering the Second Chest

When the hunter finally cracks the riddles, decodes the hidden messages, and uncovers the chest, there is an immense sense of satisfaction. The second chest, more than any other, marks the point at which the treasure hunt becomes truly immersive. The successful adventurer has pushed their limits, thought outside the box, and solved puzzles that at one point seemed impossible. This triumph is more than just the physical treasure it might contain—it is a personal victory over the challenge itself.

- **The Emotional Reward:** While the treasure chest itself may hold physical rewards, it is the emotional satisfaction of cracking the code and following the trail that offers the true reward. As with any great treasure hunt, the experience of discovery and the knowledge that one has deciphered an intricate set of clues provide an unparalleled sense of accomplishment. The thrill of solving the second chest's riddles transforms the hunter from a passive seeker into an active participant in the adventure, pushing them forward toward the ultimate goal.

- **Setting the Stage for the Final Chest:** Successfully uncovering the second chest sets the stage for even greater challenges ahead. It's a reminder that the path to treasure is never easy but requires both intellect and perseverance. The journey is far from over, and the clues, riddles, and hidden hints leading to the next chest will only become more complex as the treasure hunt nears its conclusion.

The second chest in a treasure hunt is a crucial turning point in the journey. It challenges the hunter with more intricate riddles, hidden hints, and complex clues, all while pushing their problem-solving skills to new heights. It forces the adventurer to think critically, connect different pieces of information, and utilize a wide range of knowledge and skills. The excitement of discovery, the joy of solving puzzles, and the satisfaction of uncovering hidden hints make the second chest one of the most rewarding parts of the treasure hunt.

The Third Chest

Clues, Riddles, and Hidden Hints

Clues, riddles, and hidden hints are the lifeblood of a treasure hunt, serving as the pathways through which seekers engage with the mystery and work their way toward the ultimate prize. Each clue, riddle, and hint is carefully designed to challenge the intellect, require lateral thinking, and encourage a journey of discovery, combining elements of history, logic, intuition, and perseverance. These components not only direct the treasure hunter to the next step in the quest but also enrich the entire experience, making the hunt as much about the journey as it is about the reward.

1. The Nature of Clues and Riddles

The clues and riddles of a treasure hunt are often multifaceted, drawing from a variety of fields such as literature, history, art, and geography. These riddles might be written in a straightforward form, posing a direct question or making a clear statement, or they might take the form of puzzles, wordplay, or abstract references that require deeper thinking and a greater range of knowledge to solve. Each clue and riddle serves as a stepping stone, guiding the seeker closer to the next chest or piece of the puzzle. The clues might reference historical events, famous figures, or locations, while riddles often rely on clever wordplay, numbers, or patterns.

- **Straightforward Clues:** Some clues might seem simple at first glance, perhaps a set of coordinates or an image that points towards a specific location. However, even these clues are often deceptive, containing hidden meanings or subtle elements that require deeper analysis. Straightforward clues often act as a gateway to more complex puzzles, prompting the hunter to dig deeper and think critically.

- **Cryptic Riddles:** The more cryptic riddles require the treasure hunter to think laterally, to use imagination, intuition, and lateral thinking to make connections that might not be immediately apparent. These riddles often blend historical knowledge, geography, and logic, and might involve interpreting words in more than one way or making connections between seemingly unrelated ideas. A simple phrase or sentence might contain a layer of meaning that only reveals itself upon closer inspection.

- **Pattern Recognition:** Many clues and riddles contain hidden patterns or references that the hunter must recognize to solve them. This could be a numeric pattern, a reference to a specific time or event, or even a subtle word or number hidden within the language of the riddle itself. These patterns often require the treasure hunter to think in a broader context, considering the relevance of symbols, events, or places to the overall story of the hunt.

2. Hidden Hints and Subtle Clues

The hidden hints and subtle clues are among the most tantalizing elements of a treasure hunt, as they often require keen observation, intuition, and insight to uncover. These hints are embedded within the environment, within objects or artifacts, or within the language and text of the clues themselves. The treasure hunter must pay close attention to every detail, looking for minute shifts in wording, seemingly insignificant marks, or subtle alterations in the physical surroundings. These hints often contain the critical piece of the puzzle that links one clue to another or connects to the location of the next chest.

- **Environmental Clues:** Hidden hints often come in the form of environmental details, such as the layout of the land, the positioning of landmarks, or subtle patterns in the geography. For instance, a specific arrangement of stones, the presence of a peculiar plant, or an unusual pattern in the foliage could all provide hints pointing toward the next location. The treasure hunter must learn to read the landscape as though it were a narrative, piecing together fragments of information to uncover the path forward.

- **Artifact-Based Hints:** Objects or artifacts connected to the treasure hunt can often provide valuable clues. Whether it's an old map, a piece of historical art, or a relic of a bygone era, these artifacts often contain subtle engravings, numbers, or patterns that, when carefully examined, point towards the next step. A seemingly ordinary item might hold the secret message that connects one part of the hunt to another, leading the hunter closer to their goal.

- **Symbolic and Text-Based Clues:** The language and text within clues themselves might contain subtle references or hidden meanings. This could be a passage of poetry, a line of historical writing, or an ancient inscription. These texts often require careful analysis and interpretation, making the hunt as much an intellectual challenge as a physical one. The subtlety of these clues means the hunter must engage both their mind and intuition, reading between the lines to find the true message hidden within.

3. Decoding and Problem-Solving

Decoding clues, solving riddles, and piecing together hidden hints all require a combination of critical thinking, lateral thinking, and problem-solving skills. The treasure hunter must be willing to consider multiple possibilities, to follow a trail of evidence where it leads, and to think outside of conventional boundaries. This process is often as satisfying as finding the treasure itself, as it requires not only a depth of knowledge but also creativity, patience, and perseverance. The hunter must be prepared to adapt their approach, to consider alternative interpretations of clues, and to combine different strands of information to arrive at a coherent solution.

- **Pattern Recognition and Logical Thinking:** Many of the clues and riddles within a treasure hunt are designed to test the hunter's pattern recognition skills. This could involve recognizing numerical sequences, understanding historical or geographical references, or making connections between seemingly unrelated pieces of evidence. The process often involves logical thinking and lateral problem-solving, which force the hunter to see the puzzle from multiple perspectives.

- **Persistence and Patience:** Solving riddles and uncovering hidden clues often requires persistence and patience. The treasure hunt can be a process of trial and error, where the hunter attempts various strategies, connects different pieces of information, and reevaluates clues until the solution becomes apparent. The sense of progress, even when the clues don't immediately yield their secrets, is part of the excitement of the journey.

- **Connecting the Dots:** The act of connecting disparate clues and finding a common thread that ties the pieces of the puzzle together is one of the most satisfying aspects of the treasure hunt. This requires not just intellect, but a combination of lateral thinking, creative problem-solving, and historical or geographical knowledge. The hunter must often step back and see the bigger picture, understanding how all the clues fit together into a coherent narrative.

4. The Reward of the Clues, Riddles, and Hidden Hints

The clues, riddles, and hidden hints are what make the treasure hunt so rewarding. They require the treasure hunter to engage in a process of intellectual and emotional challenge, pushing both mind and spirit. The act of deciphering these puzzles often feels like unravelling a story, where each clue contributes to a greater tale, linking history, culture, and adventure. The sense of satisfaction that comes from solving a particularly difficult clue or uncovering a hidden hint after hours of thinking, testing, and analyzing is incomparable.

- **Intellectual Challenge:** Each clue and riddle challenges the hunter's intellect, whether through logical deduction, lateral thinking, or historical knowledge. This intellectual engagement is part of what makes the treasure hunt so compelling, as it tests not just knowledge but creativity, imagination, and problem-solving skills.

- **Emotional Reward:** The emotional thrill of discovery—when the hunter finally uncovers a hidden hint or deciphers a riddle—is one of the greatest rewards of the treasure hunt. This feeling of triumph, of having solved a difficult puzzle, is akin to completing a quest or reaching a long-sought goal, making the journey both fulfilling and memorable.

- **A Journey of Adventure and Personal Growth:** The clues, riddles, and hidden hints not only push the boundaries of intellect but also foster personal growth, resilience, and the spirit of adventure. The hunt is as much about developing one's mindset and approach as it is about finding a physical treasure. It teaches patience, problem-solving, perseverance, and creativity—all valuable life skills that extend far beyond the confines of the hunt.

The clues, riddles, and hidden hints form the backbone of any treasure hunt, creating an engaging and intellectually stimulating puzzle that requires patience, ingenuity, and a willingness to think outside the box. Each of these elements adds to the mystery, enriching the journey and making the ultimate reward all the more satisfying. The process of deciphering the clues and unlocking the hidden hints is not just about reaching the end of the hunt—it's about the thrill of the journey itself, the challenges overcome, and the personal growth that comes with it.

The Fourth Chest

Clues, Riddles, and Hidden Hints

The fourth chest marks an exciting phase in the treasure hunt, a culmination of all the skills and knowledge the adventurer has acquired so far. The clues, riddles, and hidden hints associated with this chest are particularly challenging, carefully crafted to test the depth of the seeker's intellect and resourcefulness. At this stage, the hunter has likely grown more attuned to deciphering complex clues, but the fourth chest is designed to push the boundaries of their problem-solving abilities, requiring both critical thinking and creativity.

As with the previous chests, the clues and riddles are not just straightforward, linear problems to be solved but often involve layers of meaning, historical references, symbolic clues, and the occasional play on words or patterns. The fourth chest may introduce more abstract concepts or employ techniques like hidden symbolism, cryptography, or riddles that require lateral thinking. These clues often go beyond logic and introduce themes or historical facts that add complexity and excitement to the journey.

1. The Evolution of Complexity

The clues, riddles, and hidden hints for the fourth chest represent a natural progression in difficulty from the previous stages of the hunt. They are designed to be more cryptic, requiring the hunter to synthesize information from earlier clues and integrate them into more intricate puzzles. At this point, the hunter must use a combination of different cognitive skills: recognizing patterns, connecting seemingly unrelated ideas, understanding historical references, and reading between the lines.

- **Integration of Previous Knowledge:** The clues for the fourth chest build upon knowledge acquired in the earlier stages. The seeker will find that some of the riddles require them to revisit past locations, objects, or clues. This integration forces the hunter to engage with the journey holistically, rather than seeing each chest as an isolated challenge. They will need to recall details from earlier parts of the hunt and see how they fit into a larger narrative that has unfolded over time.

- **Sophisticated Wordplay and Symbolism:** The riddles for the fourth chest may become more abstract, relying on wordplay, metaphorical language, and symbolic representations. For example, a riddle could use a historical reference to a famous philosopher or event, with the answer lying not in the literal interpretation but in a metaphorical or philosophical context. The treasure hunter must become familiar with recognizing how language can function in unexpected ways, requiring a flexible, creative approach to solve the riddle.

- **Cryptographic Challenges:** Some clues could involve cryptographic puzzles that require decryption, possibly involving ciphers or encoding techniques like the Caesar cipher or more complex cryptographic methods. These types of clues add an intellectual layer to the hunt, where the hunter must decipher hidden messages embedded within a text or image.

2. Hidden Hints in the Environment

At this stage of the treasure hunt, hidden hints become even more elusive, demanding an acute sense of observation and a deeper connection to the surroundings. Hidden hints may no longer be obvious symbols or artifacts but rather subtle environmental cues, reflections, or details embedded in the landscape that point the hunter in the right direction. The seeker must begin to read their environment like a map, paying attention to every detail, from the arrangement of objects to the way light and shadow fall in a particular place.

- **Environmental Cues:** Environmental clues might come in the form of the arrangement of natural elements, such as specific rock formations, tree patterns, or even the way a river curves or intersects with a landmark. These geographical features can hint at where the chest might be hidden. The treasure hunter will need to study the landscape with an eye for detail, recognizing patterns that have significance in the context of the hunt.

- **Shadows, Reflections, and Light:** The play of light and shadow could provide essential clues. At specific times of day, the position of the sun might reveal hidden messages or point toward a location of interest. For example, the shadow of an object might align with a specific point on a map, or a reflection in a body of water could reveal a hidden inscription or coordinate. This requires not only observation but an understanding of how natural elements work together to reveal something that may have been concealed in plain sight.

- **Subtle Alterations in the Environment:** Sometimes, hidden hints are embedded in the very fabric of the environment. A seemingly unimportant detail, like a missing stone or an unusually placed object, could be a deliberate clue. These alterations are meant to guide the treasure hunter along the correct path, but they require a deep attentiveness to the world around them. The hunter must be able to recognize that even the smallest shift in the environment can have significance.

3. Decoding the Hidden Messages

Decoding the clues and unraveling the hidden hints in the fourth chest often requires an advanced level of analysis and interpretation. The hunter must engage in a process of synthesis, taking all the information they've gathered so far and making connections between the riddles, the history, the geography, and the subtle environmental cues. The clues may no longer be solved using a single approach but instead require the treasure hunter to think creatively and bring together disparate ideas in a cohesive way.

- **Pattern Recognition Across Multiple Clues:** As the clues become more intricate, the ability to recognize patterns becomes increasingly important. The treasure hunter must not only spot individual patterns but also look for broader thematic connections across the entire set of clues. This could involve recognizing recurring motifs, symbols, or references to particular historical periods or events that tie everything together.

- **Historical and Cultural Insights:** In many treasure hunts, the clues will reference historical figures, events, or periods, and understanding these references is crucial to solving the puzzle. The fourth chest might introduce a more complex layer of history or culture that requires the hunter to think beyond the immediate present. This could involve decoding an ancient reference, understanding the significance of a specific historical figure, or making connections between cultural symbols that have deeper meanings.

- **Theories and Hypotheses:** As the clues become more complex, the treasure hunter might need to form hypotheses and test them against the available clues. This process of trial and error allows the adventurer to narrow down the possibilities and uncover hidden truths. However, it also requires a degree of flexibility—when one theory doesn't work, the hunter must be ready to abandon it and pursue a different line of thinking.

4. The Sense of Reward

The fourth chest is a pivotal moment in the treasure hunt, not just because of the treasure it may hold but because of the mental and emotional satisfaction that comes from solving complex puzzles. Successfully deciphering the riddles, connecting the environmental clues, and uncovering the hidden hints brings a sense of accomplishment and progress. The treasure hunter realizes that they are now closer than ever to reaching the final chest, and that the journey itself, with all its challenges and discoveries, is the true reward.

- **Intellectual Achievement:** Decoding the clues for the fourth chest brings a sense of intellectual achievement. Each riddle solved, each pattern uncovered, and each hidden hint discovered is a testament to the hunter's growing knowledge and skills. The challenge intensifies, but so does the sense of triumph, as the adventurer's abilities are put to the test in increasingly sophisticated ways.

- **Building Momentum:** The successful discovery of the fourth chest sets the stage for the final phase of the hunt. The clues have become more difficult, but the treasure hunter's experience has also evolved. With each chest, the adventurer builds more confidence, and the momentum towards the final prize grows stronger.

- **Reflection and Reward:** After overcoming the challenges of the fourth chest, the treasure hunter reflects on the path they've taken. The journey is no longer just about finding the treasure—it's about the mental and emotional growth that comes with solving puzzles, discovering hidden meanings, and engaging with history and mystery. The process itself becomes the ultimate reward, and the treasure now feels like the inevitable conclusion to a deeply rewarding journey.

The fourth chest represents a turning point in the treasure hunt. The clues, riddles, and hidden hints are more challenging and abstract than ever before, requiring the treasure hunter to think creatively, make connections across different realms of knowledge, and engage deeply with their environment. At this stage, the adventurer is not just solving problems—they are building a richer understanding of the world and honing their ability to think critically and intuitively. The fourth chest is a milestone that sets the stage for the final steps of the hunt, where the culmination of all the intellectual and physical challenges comes to fruition.

The Fifth Chest

Clues, Riddles, and Hidden Hints

The fifth and final chest in this treasure hunt is the ultimate test of all the skills and knowledge you've gathered throughout your journey. By now, you have grown accustomed to deciphering complex clues, navigating challenges, and thinking outside the box. However, the final chest will push you even further, as the clues, riddles, and hidden hints are designed to test not only your intellect but your creativity, intuition, and perseverance. This is the culmination of everything—the reward for those who have successfully navigated the intricate puzzles and obstacles of the hunt.

1. A Complex Web of Clues

Unlike the previous chests, the clues for the fifth chest may not come in a straightforward or linear fashion. The final challenge often involves multiple layers of meaning, requiring a more sophisticated approach to deciphering. The clues could involve a combination of historical references, symbolic language, and encoded messages, all of which need to be pieced together in a careful and methodical manner. The hunter must navigate through a complex web of ideas, drawing connections between seemingly unrelated pieces of information.

- **Symbolism and Metaphor:** The final chest is likely to involve deeper symbolic meaning, where the clues are not just about finding a literal answer but about interpreting the hidden symbolism behind the riddles. These clues may reference mythology, literature, or cultural symbols that require a broader understanding of human history and thought. The hunter will need to engage with these abstract clues and interpret them through a more philosophical or metaphorical lens.

- **Abstract Puzzles and Lateral Thinking:** The riddles for the fifth chest may require lateral thinking—solving the problem by stepping outside the usual logical framework. Expect puzzles that demand creative solutions and thinking that breaks the traditional mold. Some clues may appear to have no direct answer, but with careful observation and a shift in perspective, their meanings will unfold.

- **Multidimensional Clues:** The final chest may involve multi-dimensional clues, where you have to look at things from different angles. For example, the clue may be hidden within a physical artifact that requires the interpretation of light, shadow, or reflection. Alternatively, clues could be scattered across different locations or types of media (such as maps, journals, objects, or coded messages), requiring you to piece them together to unlock the final solution.

2. Environmental and Contextual Hints

At this point in the treasure hunt, the environment plays a crucial role in uncovering hidden clues. The hunter must rely on their keen observation skills, noticing the smallest details in the surroundings that may offer subtle guidance. Environmental hints are often intertwined with the physical world, making the treasure hunt as much about exploration and discovery as it is about solving puzzles.

- **Geographic Features and Landmarks:** The location of the fifth chest is likely marked by unique geographical features or landmarks. Clues may involve coordinates or symbolic references to the terrain itself. A specific tree, rock formation, or landmark may hold the key to understanding where the chest lies hidden. Understanding the geography of the area and the natural features that surround it can provide essential insights.

- **Changes in the Environment:** Hidden hints may also lie in how the environment changes at specific times of day or under certain conditions. For example, the sun might illuminate a hidden symbol at dawn, or the position of the stars at night could offer clues that guide you. A hidden inscription might only be visible under a certain angle or when sunlight hits it in a particular way. This calls for sharp awareness and patience, as you might need to wait for the right moment to uncover these subtle clues.

- **Symbolic Placement:** The location and arrangement of objects in the environment may also be part of the clue system. An object placed out of its natural context or a slight alteration to the surroundings could be a deliberate hint that directs the treasure hunter to the chest's precise location. As with previous chests, the key to understanding these hints is observation—every small detail counts.

3. Deeper Historical and Cultural References

The clues in the fifth chest often rely on a deep understanding of history, culture, and sometimes even specific mythologies. These references may not be immediately obvious and could require knowledge of specific figures, events, or ideologies that are relevant to the puzzle. A reference to a historical artifact, a forgotten myth, or a lost civilization could be the very clue you need to unlock the final chest.

- **Historical Figures and Events:** The fifth chest may involve references to significant figures from history—individuals whose actions or creations are linked to the final treasure. These could include well-known figures such as explorers, scholars, or artists whose work has had a lasting cultural impact. Understanding their lives, contributions, and connections to the theme of the treasure hunt could be crucial in solving the final riddles.

- **Cultural and Mythological Contexts:** Ancient myths, folktales, and cultural traditions often provide rich sources of clues for treasure hunts. The fifth chest may reference specific mythological stories or allegorical symbols that require familiarity with various cultural legends. These references may not be direct but could form part of a broader narrative that leads to the final discovery.

- **Philosophical or Intellectual Themes:** Clues for the fifth chest may delve into deeper philosophical or intellectual ideas, requiring a more abstract interpretation. The riddles could reference specific philosophies, schools of thought, or ethical dilemmas that challenge the treasure hunter to think beyond the tangible and engage with larger concepts. Solving these clues requires critical thinking and a broad intellectual understanding.

4. The Sense of Finality and Reward

As you approach the final chest, the excitement builds—not just because of the treasure itself, but because you are close to completing a long and difficult journey. The clues, riddles, and hidden hints that lead to the fifth chest are designed to reward you for your persistence, creativity, and intellectual growth. They provide a sense of closure to the puzzle while also offering a final layer of complexity and challenge. Solving the last puzzle, deciphering the final clue, and reaching the chest is both an intellectual triumph and a deeply rewarding emotional experience.

- **The Ultimate Test of Skill and Patience:** The clues for the fifth chest are the ultimate test of your abilities as a treasure hunter. Every skill you've developed—whether it's problem-solving, creative thinking, historical knowledge, or attention to detail—comes into play as you work to unlock the final chest. This is where the lessons from earlier stages truly come together, and your persistence pays off. The reward is not just the treasure but the personal growth that comes from overcoming such a demanding challenge.

- **The Final Puzzle:** Solving the final riddle is like piecing together a puzzle that has taken years to complete. The satisfaction of finally cracking the code, understanding the hidden meaning, and locating the treasure chest will be immense. But the journey has already enriched you—through the clues, riddles, and hidden hints, you will have learned lessons about patience, persistence, and creative problem-solving that will last a lifetime.

- **A Sense of Completion:** Reaching the fifth chest brings a sense of profound completion. It is the end of one journey and the beginning of another, where the skills you've acquired can now be applied to new challenges. The final chest may be the most difficult to unlock, but it also serves as a testament to the seeker's growth and determination, offering a fitting conclusion to the treasure hunt.

The clues, riddles, and hidden hints leading to the fifth chest are the pinnacle of the treasure hunt. As you face the final chest, the journey has become a test of everything you have learned and experienced up until now. The complexities of the clues will demand creative and lateral thinking, deep historical and cultural knowledge, and a sharp eye for detail. However, overcoming these challenges will reward you with not only the treasure itself but also the immense satisfaction of completing one of the most intellectually and emotionally enriching quests of your life. The fifth chest marks the ultimate conclusion of the hunt, a crowning achievement in a journey of discovery, growth, and triumph.

What This Treasure Hunt Means

Inspiring a Nation to Dream Again

The treasure hunt isn't just about hidden chests, riddles, and the rewards waiting at the end of the journey. It's about something deeper—a spark that ignites the imagination and rekindles a sense of wonder in people. This treasure hunt, like many of its kind throughout history, has the power to inspire a nation to dream again. It's about reconnecting with that childlike sense of adventure and possibility, where the world is full of untapped wonders, and anything feels possible if you dare to seek it.

1. Reawakening the Spirit of Adventure

For many, adulthood often comes with a sense of routine and limitations. Dreams and desires, once vivid and limitless, can fade away under the pressures of responsibility and practicality. But treasure hunts, with their inherent mysteries and calls to explore, offer a reminder that there's more to life than the daily grind. The challenge of seeking out treasure brings with it a return to the spirit of adventure, that innate desire to chase something greater than ourselves.

This treasure hunt reminds us of the adventures of the past—of explorers who ventured into the unknown, of pioneers who braved uncertainty, and of the thrill that came with the idea of discovery. It ignites a fire in the heart of those who participate and those who simply hear the stories of the brave souls embarking on the quest. As people from all walks of life engage with the riddles and stories, it revives a sense of possibility and excitement. Whether young or old, those who dare to dream are reminded that life can still be full of excitement, mystery, and the thrill of the unknown.

2. Bringing Hope and Purpose

In times of uncertainty or struggle, a treasure hunt can bring more than just the pursuit of a physical object. It brings hope—a belief that something greater lies ahead. The excitement surrounding a treasure hunt offers an escape from the challenges of everyday life. It becomes a way for individuals to set aside their worries and come together to chase something bigger than themselves.

Inspiring a nation to dream again isn't just about offering a material prize; it's about restoring the belief that there are meaningful things worth striving for. A treasure hunt with high stakes and intricate clues creates a sense of purpose and direction, motivating individuals to persevere through challenges and setbacks. The path to the treasure is never easy, and it reflects the greater journey of life itself: full of hurdles, but with the promise of reward for those who keep going. It serves as a metaphor for life—an ongoing quest where success isn't just about the destination but about the lessons learned and the growth that occurs along the way.

3. Uniting People Through a Shared Vision

A treasure hunt has the unique power to bring people together. It can unite communities, families, friends, and even strangers, all chasing after the same dream. In a nation, when people participate in such a quest, they are not just working towards their own personal gain but are involved in a collective pursuit. Each clue solved, each step taken, is part of a greater shared experience, a connection between individuals who are all bound by the same goal.

This collective experience fosters collaboration, teamwork, and a sense of unity. It breaks down barriers and creates bonds among people who may not otherwise have had a chance to interact. The treasure hunt becomes a rallying point—a cause that transcends individual differences, where people come together to engage in something greater than themselves. In a world that can often feel fragmented, a treasure hunt like this can serve as a reminder that we all share common dreams and aspirations, and that working together is how we move forward.

4. Encouraging Curiosity and Lifelong Learning

One of the key lessons that treasure hunts impart is the value of curiosity. As hunters engage with the riddles and historical clues, they are constantly learning, expanding their horizons, and discovering new things about the world around them. This process of exploration encourages people to ask questions, seek answers, and challenge themselves intellectually.

A treasure hunt taps into our innate curiosity, inviting individuals to step out of their comfort zones and explore new ideas, places, and perspectives. The hunt for the treasure is not only a search for riches but also a journey of personal discovery. It encourages participants to view the world with a fresh perspective, to look at ordinary things in an extraordinary way, and to engage with history, science, and culture in new and exciting ways.

Inspiring a nation to dream again also means encouraging a society that values learning, growth, and the pursuit of knowledge. The treasure hunt fosters this mindset, as individuals are asked to apply their intelligence, creativity, and critical thinking to solve the mysteries at hand. As the hunt unfolds, it becomes clear that the real treasure lies not in the chest itself, but in the knowledge and experiences gained along the way. This sense of intellectual discovery can reignite a passion for learning that extends far beyond the treasure hunt itself.

5. Sparking the Imagination

Treasure hunts encourage participants to think beyond the ordinary and imagine the impossible. The clues and riddles often require a leap of faith, a shift in perspective, and a willingness to embrace the unknown. This engagement with the unknown fosters creativity and sparks the imagination, reminding us all that reality is often more flexible and wondrous than we might think.

The act of dreaming about what might be hidden within the chests—the possibilities that await—brings a sense of magic into the lives of those who take part in the hunt. The stories and legends of treasure hunts throughout history—real or imagined— offer the perfect backdrop for this imaginative exploration. The clues themselves might suggest connections to ancient civilizations, lost worlds, or undiscovered artifacts. In imagining what could be, individuals are inspired to think about the future, to dream about what might be possible in their own lives, and to tap into their own creative potential.

This spark of imagination isn't limited to the participants of the hunt; it extends to the broader community. As people hear about the treasure hunt and follow its progress, they are swept up in the excitement and wonder of what's to come. This creates a ripple effect that spreads across the nation, inspiring others to think bigger, to pursue their own dreams, and to embrace the possibilities that lie ahead.

6. A New Generation of Dreamers

One of the most lasting impacts of a treasure hunt like this is its ability to inspire the next generation. Children who hear about the adventure will grow up with a sense of possibility, believing that the world is full of mystery and wonder to be discovered. For young minds, the treasure hunt shows that anything is achievable with curiosity, determination, and creativity. It instills in them the belief that they, too, can embark on their own great adventures, solve complex problems, and make their mark on the world.

As these children grow up, they'll carry with them the lessons of the treasure hunt—of never giving up, of chasing after something larger than life, and of believing in their ability to succeed against the odds. The treasure hunt becomes a cultural touchstone, a story that is passed down through generations, continuing to inspire and spark the imaginations of those who hear it.

Inspiring a nation to dream again is not just about offering a prize or creating a moment of excitement. It's about tapping into something fundamental within all of us—the desire to explore, to learn, and to imagine. A treasure hunt does more than reveal hidden chests; it reveals the hidden potential within each of us to discover something greater than ourselves. By embarking on a quest that challenges the mind, engages the heart, and fuels the imagination, we can all become part of a larger, shared dream. The treasure hunt offers a renewed belief in the impossible, encouraging individuals and communities to dream bigger, work together, and create a future that is rich with possibility.

The Joy of Giving Back

At its core, the treasure hunt is not only about the thrill of discovery or the reward of finding priceless treasures, but also about the profound joy that comes from giving back. The journey is about more than just what is hidden in the chests; it's about the ways in which the process can enrich the lives of others, inspire generosity, and leave a lasting legacy that extends beyond the boundaries of the hunt itself. The act of giving back—whether through sharing the experience, supporting others, or contributing to the greater good—adds a deeper layer of fulfillment to the adventure.

1. Creating a Ripple Effect of Generosity

While the treasure hunt may start with the pursuit of material rewards, the process often fosters a sense of generosity that goes far beyond personal gain. The excitement and challenge of the hunt draw individuals together, creating a sense of community and shared purpose. As participants and onlookers get involved in the search, the act of sharing information, offering encouragement, and helping fellow hunters along the way becomes a central aspect of the experience.

There's a unique joy that comes from sharing discoveries—whether it's a breakthrough in solving a riddle, a moment of realization, or even the subtle clues that can guide others in their search. Instead of keeping the pursuit entirely to oneself, treasure hunters often feel compelled to give back to others, sharing their insights and supporting one another in ways that create a sense of camaraderie. This collective spirit enriches the journey, as it encourages individuals to lift one another up rather than compete in isolation.

This sharing of knowledge and encouragement spreads outward, creating a ripple effect of generosity. It reminds us that life's greatest rewards are often not found in individual success but in how we help and inspire others to reach their potential. The treasure hunt, in this way, becomes an act of collective giving—not only in terms of material wealth but in the sharing of experiences, wisdom, and support.

2. Giving Back to the Community

Another powerful aspect of the treasure hunt is its potential to give back to communities. Many treasure hunts, both real and symbolic, are designed to benefit others beyond the treasure hunters themselves. Whether through charitable donations, public goods, or community-driven projects, treasure hunts can serve as vehicles for positive social impact.

For example, some hunts encourage participants to contribute a portion of their winnings to a charitable cause or donate time and resources to those in need. The treasure hunt can become an opportunity to make a tangible difference in the world, offering not just personal fulfillment but the chance to improve the lives of others.

As participants engage in the hunt, they are reminded that the joy of discovery is not just personal—it can also be communal. The knowledge and wealth discovered during the hunt can be redirected to benefit others, whether it's funding local projects, supporting educational initiatives, or contributing to the welfare of underprivileged groups. The joy of giving back is seen not just in the treasures unearthed, but in how those treasures are used to bring joy, opportunity, and improvement to the lives of others.

The act of giving back in this way can turn a personal adventure into a shared one, where the joy of victory is magnified by the positive change it brings to the world.

3. The Power of Legacy

One of the most profound aspects of the treasure hunt—and the act of giving back—is the legacy that it leaves behind. Treasures and rewards are fleeting, but the impact of a well-intended act of giving can last for generations. The wealth or valuable items discovered in the hunt may eventually fade, but the lessons learned and the goodwill created will continue to reverberate.

When participants give back, whether by donating to charity or simply sharing the experience with others, they are not just enriching their own lives—they are creating a legacy of generosity that can inspire others long after the hunt ends. The joy of giving back, in this sense, becomes an enduring force that can influence future generations. Those who benefit from this spirit of giving are not only grateful but motivated to continue the cycle of generosity and service to others.

By fostering a culture of giving, treasure hunts can create lasting legacies that transcend material wealth. The intangible rewards—such as the joy of helping others, the satisfaction of contributing to a greater cause, and the inspiration to continue the cycle of generosity—become the true treasures of the hunt. These legacies of kindness, generosity, and community-mindedness are passed down, creating a ripple effect that continues far beyond the treasure hunters themselves.

4. The Inner Fulfillment of Helping Others

One of the most rewarding aspects of giving back is the profound sense of inner fulfillment that comes from helping others. There is a unique joy in watching someone else succeed, especially when you've played a role in their success. This sense of fulfillment is not limited to financial rewards or recognition; it often comes from the quiet satisfaction of knowing that you've made a difference in someone else's life.

Whether it's offering advice to a fellow hunter, volunteering your time to organize the hunt, or simply being part of a team that works together to solve clues, the act of giving back fills the heart with a sense of purpose and accomplishment. The joy that comes from helping others is often deeper and more lasting than the thrill of finding the treasure itself. The treasure hunt becomes a celebration not just of individual success, but of collective achievement and the shared joy of community.

This sense of fulfillment strengthens the bonds between people and encourages an ethos of generosity that extends far beyond the hunt itself. It reinforces the idea that life's greatest rewards are often found in the connections we build with others, and the ways in which we can contribute to something larger than ourselves.

5. The Legacy of Inspiration and Empowerment

Finally, the joy of giving back is tied to the empowerment it brings to others. When people give, they not only help those in need, but they also inspire others to do the same. A treasure hunt, particularly one that encourages participants to give back, can become a platform for empowerment—empowering individuals to believe in their own potential and encouraging them to pay it forward.

Through their actions, participants demonstrate that everyone has the power to make a positive impact. Whether it's offering a helping hand to someone who is struggling with a particular clue or contributing a portion of their winnings to a charitable organization, the act of giving becomes a powerful statement of belief in the greater good. This ripple effect of empowerment spreads to those who may have once felt powerless or disconnected, reminding them that they too can make a difference in the world.

When people see the results of giving back—whether through personal connections, community improvements, or positive change in society—they are inspired to take action themselves. The treasure hunt, in this way, serves as a catalyst for a larger movement of empowerment, inspiring others to follow in the footsteps of those who have made a difference. The joy of giving back becomes a guiding principle, one that empowers individuals and communities to continually strive for betterment, both for themselves and for the world around them.

The joy of giving back is one of the most transformative and enriching aspects of any adventure, and the treasure hunt is no exception. Through acts of generosity, the sharing of knowledge, and the use of newfound wealth to benefit others, the hunt creates a cycle of giving that extends beyond personal rewards. It fosters community, strengthens relationships, and empowers individuals to create lasting legacies of positive change. As the treasure hunt continues, it inspires others to dream, to give, and to create a world that is richer not only in treasures but in the connections that bind us all together. The true treasure of the hunt, then, is not just what we find, but what we are able to give back to the world.

The Author's Journey

What the Hunt Taught Me

The treasure hunt was more than just a search for riches or a race against time to uncover hidden treasures—it was an invaluable journey of personal discovery. In the midst of cryptic clues, historical riddles, and the challenges of navigating an unpredictable quest, I learned lessons that reshaped my perspective on life, problem-solving, and the very essence of what it means to pursue something meaningful. Looking back on the five-year journey that brought this adventure to life, I've realized how much it taught me—not only about treasure hunting but about life itself.

1. The Power of Patience

The first and most profound lesson I learned was the importance of patience. A treasure hunt is not a sprint; it's a marathon, and there are no shortcuts. As I worked through complex puzzles, consulted experts, and spent countless hours searching for the right clues, I quickly realized that there would be no immediate gratification. Success didn't come overnight, and neither did the answers to the riddles.

Each clue I encountered led to more questions, and often I would reach a dead end, only to start over again with a new perspective. What I came to understand was that patience is not just about waiting—it's about persistence, about continuing to move forward even when the path seems unclear. The hunt taught me that success often requires time and that the most rewarding moments are those that come after long periods of effort and quiet perseverance.

2. Embracing Uncertainty and Adaptability

One of the greatest lessons I learned through the hunt was the ability to embrace uncertainty. The nature of treasure hunting is unpredictable; no matter how well you plan or prepare, things will rarely go according to the script. The journey is filled with twists and turns, moments of doubt, and sudden revelations. In those moments, I realized that my success wasn't determined by how well I had planned, but by my ability to adapt to the unexpected.

I learned to pivot when faced with obstacles, to adjust my thinking when a clue didn't make sense, and to approach problems from multiple angles. It became clear to me that adaptability is a key skill not only in treasure hunting but in life. In order to find success, you need to stay flexible, open to change, and ready to face whatever challenges come your way. This mindset of embracing uncertainty and remaining agile has stayed with me in all areas of my life, reminding me that there is always room for growth, no matter how daunting the unknown might seem.

3. The Importance of Collaboration

At the beginning of the hunt, I thought that the journey was a solo quest. After all, I was the one who created the treasure map, designed the riddles, and set the stage for the adventure. However, as the journey unfolded, it became clear that the real power of the hunt lay in collaboration. There was no way to navigate the complexities of the clues and puzzles alone. Whether it was working with a team of experts to decipher historical references, discussing theories with other hunters, or simply receiving encouragement from those who believed in the cause, I quickly realized that treasure hunting is never a solitary pursuit. It's a collective effort that thrives on shared knowledge, diverse perspectives, and mutual support.

The hunt taught me that collaboration is a strength. It's through teamwork that we can accomplish things we might never have been able to do on our own. People bring unique skills, knowledge, and insights that can make all the difference in solving complex problems. In the end, the shared joy of discovery—whether it was cracking a difficult riddle or finding a hidden chest—was more rewarding because it was experienced together. This lesson in collaboration has shaped my approach to both work and personal life, reminding me that working together can often lead to far greater results than going it alone.

4. Problem-Solving as a Journey, Not a Destination

Through every twist, turn, and puzzle of the treasure hunt, I learned to embrace the art of problem-solving in a new light. It's easy to think of problem-solving as a linear process, where each step is a straightforward solution that leads to the final answer. But in treasure hunting, I quickly learned that problem-solving is rarely so simple. It's a creative, iterative process that involves trial and error, constant reevaluation, and a willingness to take risks.

Each clue I encountered felt like a puzzle within a puzzle, and many times, the solution wasn't immediately apparent. But the process itself—of engaging with the challenge, thinking outside the box, and experimenting with different approaches—became its own reward. The hunt taught me that problem-solving is not about finding the perfect answer as quickly as possible, but about enjoying the process of discovery and being open to unexpected solutions.

This approach to problem-solving has translated into my personal and professional life. Whether faced with a difficult decision or a new challenge, I now see the value in the journey of finding a solution, not just the destination. It's in this journey that we grow, learn, and discover new ways to think and act.

5. The Value of Small Wins

During the treasure hunt, there were moments when progress felt slow, when the end goal seemed distant, or when it felt like I was taking one step forward and two steps back. But even in those moments of frustration, I learned the value of small wins. Every time I cracked a piece of a riddle, found a clue that led me in the right direction, or even just gained a deeper understanding of the puzzle at hand, I celebrated those small victories.

These moments of progress were crucial for maintaining motivation and keeping momentum. They reminded me that success is not just the grand final moment of discovery, but the accumulation of many smaller steps along the way. Each small win adds up, and these little victories often provide the momentum needed to push forward, even when the road ahead feels long.

This lesson has had a lasting impact. In my personal and professional life, I've learned to celebrate the small achievements, whether it's completing a difficult project, learning something new, or simply making it through a challenging week. These small wins give us the strength and determination to keep going, even when the bigger goals seem out of reach.

6. The Importance of Giving Back

One of the most significant lessons the treasure hunt taught me was the importance of giving back. As the hunt progressed and the treasure began to take shape, I realized that the ultimate value of the treasure was not in the physical objects, but in the impact they could have on the world. Whether through charitable donations, sharing knowledge, or supporting the community, the true treasure lies in the ways we can use our discoveries to help others.

The journey taught me that success is not just about accumulating wealth or achievements for oneself, but about using those successes to make a positive difference in the lives of others. The joy of giving back, of contributing to a greater cause, has been one of the most rewarding aspects of the hunt. It has reshaped my perspective on wealth, success, and fulfillment. The real treasure, I came to realize, is found not in the chest itself but in how we use what we have to inspire and uplift those around us.

7. Embracing the Unexpected

Finally, the treasure hunt taught me to embrace the unexpected. Whether it was an unanticipated breakthrough, a chance encounter with an expert, or an unplanned detour that led to a key piece of the puzzle, the hunt was full of surprises. What I learned from this was that life is full of unpredictability, and often, it's the unexpected moments that bring the greatest rewards.

The ability to stay open to the unexpected, to adjust to new information, and to embrace surprises with a sense of curiosity and excitement is something that has stayed with me long after the treasure hunt ended. It's a reminder that life's greatest opportunities often come when we least expect them and that sometimes, the most meaningful discoveries happen outside of our plans.

The treasure hunt taught me many lessons—patience, problem-solving, collaboration, adaptability, and the value of giving back. But perhaps the most significant lesson was that the journey itself, with all of its challenges, uncertainties, and small victories, is as valuable as the treasure at the end. The skills, insights, and personal growth gained along the way are the true rewards of the hunt. As I reflect on this five-year adventure, I am grateful for the lessons it has imparted, for they have shaped me into someone who is not only a better problem-solver but also a more empathetic, adaptable, and generous individual.

Reflections on Five Years of Creation

Looking back on the five-year journey that led to the creation of this treasure hunt, I find myself immersed in a blend of awe, gratitude, and introspection. What began as an ambitious idea evolved into an experience that shaped my thinking, tested my patience, and forced me to confront challenges that I never anticipated. The process of designing this treasure hunt, crafting the riddles, curating the prizes, and collaborating with experts was far more than just an intellectual challenge—it was a transformative experience that reshaped my understanding of creativity, perseverance, and the power of dreams.

1. The Spark of an Idea

Five years ago, this project began with nothing more than a spark of an idea—a vision of an elaborate treasure hunt that would captivate the imagination of individuals from all walks of life. What excited me most was the idea of creating something interactive, dynamic, and filled with mystery—something that would inspire people to engage with history, explore the unknown, and experience the joy of discovery.

At the outset, the concept was simple: create a challenge with hidden treasures that could not be found without great thought and determination. But as the idea began to take shape, it became clear that this would require more than just a treasure map and a set of clues. It would need a story, a narrative that connected the hunt to deeper themes of exploration, personal growth, and legacy. The idea evolved into something grander—a journey that not only sought to uncover material treasures but also to spark personal transformation.

The spark of an idea often seems small and manageable, but over time, it grows into something far more complex. The treasure hunt became a living entity, an intricate web of clues and puzzles, designed to push boundaries, spark curiosity, and challenge participants in ways they had never experienced before.

2. The Design of the Hunt: Challenges and Surprises

Creating the hunt was far more challenging than I initially anticipated. Each clue had to be carefully designed to lead participants through an intellectual maze—one that would test their reasoning, creativity, and perseverance. Early on, I learned that designing a treasure hunt wasn't just about making the puzzles hard; it was about making them engaging, fair, and rewarding. The difficulty of the hunt had to strike the right balance—it needed to be tough enough to challenge even the most experienced treasure hunters but not so obscure that it would frustrate participants.

There were moments when the puzzles didn't work as I envisioned, or when an intended clue became too difficult or confusing. These moments of setback were humbling. I found myself revising and reworking, asking myself: "Is this too easy?" or "Is this too hard?" But with each revision, the process became more and more enriching. I learned that creativity isn't a straight line, but a winding road with unexpected detours and discoveries.

Perhaps the most surprising lesson I encountered was the importance of storytelling in the hunt's design. As I crafted the riddles and clues, I realized that they weren't just isolated tasks to be completed. They were part of a larger narrative—a story that would captivate the imaginations of the participants. The treasure hunt wasn't just about finding a chest; it was about immersing people in a journey, about allowing them to feel like they were part of something greater than themselves. The narrative became as important as the puzzles themselves.

Creating a seamless story took time, patience, and careful planning. It involved not only designing the clues but also weaving in the historical and personal significance behind the treasures. I had to consider the emotional journey participants would undergo—the highs and lows of their progress, the challenges they would face, and the eventual thrill of discovery.

3. Collaborating with Experts: A Humbling Experience

One of the most enriching parts of the process was working with a wide array of experts from different fields. While I had the vision and the idea for the treasure hunt, I quickly realized that the complexity of the riddles, the historical depth of the artifacts, and the sheer scale of the project required collaboration. I needed experts in history, art, cryptography, and even geography—people who could help shape the elements of the hunt and provide valuable insights.

Working alongside these specialists was a humbling experience. I learned that creating something truly meaningful requires more than just one person's vision. It takes a team of individuals who each bring their own knowledge, skills, and expertise to the table. This collaboration taught me the value of diverse perspectives and how essential it is to listen to those who know more than you in their respective fields. Each conversation with an expert—whether a historian detailing the background of a rare artifact or a cryptographer helping me craft a particularly tricky puzzle—enriched my understanding of the hunt's components and made the treasure hunt more authentic and compelling.

Through these collaborations, I also came to realize that the true value of a project like this lies not in what it accomplishes for you personally, but in how it contributes to the community of people involved. The knowledge and insights shared by experts became an integral part of the project's success, reminding me that no great endeavor is achieved alone.

4. The Unexpected Personal Growth

While the hunt was about creating a thrilling experience for others, I found that it was also a journey of personal growth for me. As the project progressed, I experienced moments of doubt, frustration, and even self-questioning. There were times when the clues weren't coming together, when deadlines loomed large, and when I felt as though I was in over my head.

But it was through those moments of struggle that I grew the most. I had to learn to trust the process and to lean into the discomfort that comes with creativity. The treasure hunt taught me the value of persistence and the importance of trusting that things would eventually fall into place if I kept moving forward. I learned to embrace failure not as an end, but as part of the learning process. Each setback was an opportunity to reassess, reevaluate, and grow.

The journey taught me that success isn't just about achieving the goal—it's about the lessons learned along the way, the resilience developed through challenges, and the personal growth that happens when you push beyond your limits. The hunt became a mirror for my own transformation, forcing me to confront my own limitations and, in the process, discover my capacity for creativity, problem-solving, and perseverance.

5. The Impact of the Hunt: Reflections on Legacy

As the treasure hunt took shape, I began to see its potential impact beyond just the participants. What started as a personal project evolved into something much larger—a movement that could inspire people to think creatively, to embrace adventure, and to rediscover the joy of exploration. I began to see the hunt not just as a game, but as a legacy—a gift that would spark curiosity in others, challenge them to grow, and leave a lasting mark on those who took part.

In these final stages of the hunt's creation, I've come to understand the importance of leaving a legacy that endures beyond a single event. This treasure hunt, with all of its riddles, challenges, and stories, is part of something bigger—something that encourages exploration, ignites passion, and inspires others to continue the journey. As I reflect on the five years of creation, I realize that the true value of this experience lies not just in the treasure that will be found, but in the spark of curiosity it ignites, the challenges it presents, and the inspiration it leaves behind for future adventurers.

The five-year journey of creating this treasure hunt has been an incredibly rewarding experience—one that has reshaped my understanding of creativity, collaboration, and personal growth. The process has been filled with challenges, but it has also been a journey of discovery, not only of hidden treasures but of the untapped potential within myself and others. The hunt has taught me that the pursuit of something meaningful takes time, dedication, and a willingness to embrace uncertainty and failure. It has shown me that true treasure is not always found in the end result, but in the growth, learning, and relationships formed along the way. As the treasure hunt nears its conclusion, I am filled with gratitude for the lessons learned, the people who have joined me on this journey, and the legacy that will continue long after the last clue is solved.

Carrying the Torch Forward

Maintaining the Tradition of Exploration

As the treasure hunt draws to a close, it is clear that the real treasure isn't the gold or the priceless artifacts, but the enduring legacy of exploration that this journey has created. The spirit of discovery, the joy of unraveling mysteries, and the drive to push boundaries—these are the lasting effects of the hunt. And now, as we look to the future, the question becomes: How do we continue this legacy of exploration?

The beauty of exploration lies in its endless potential. It's not limited to the hunt for material riches, nor does it need to involve a specific set of clues or a particular destination. Exploration is a mindset, a way of engaging with the world that encourages curiosity, challenges assumptions, and fosters innovation. As this treasure hunt has demonstrated, there is no shortage of new frontiers to explore—whether in the realm of history, science, or personal development. And it is this mindset that must be passed on to future generations, inspiring them to carry the torch forward.

1. Inspiring Future Explorers

The first step in continuing the legacy of exploration is inspiring the next generation of adventurers, thinkers, and problem-solvers. This treasure hunt, though it may seem like a fun and thrilling game, serves as a metaphor for the way exploration shapes lives. It shows that exploration is not about taking the easy path but about seeking out the unknown and overcoming obstacles along the way. The hunt, with its riddles, clues, and historical references, has been a test of intellect, perseverance, and creativity.

By sharing the story of this treasure hunt and its challenges, we can motivate others to seek out their own adventures—whether that means exploring the depths of history, charting new territories, or solving complex problems. The legacy of this hunt can serve as a model for future explorers, showing them that there is always something new to uncover, whether in the world around us or within ourselves.

2. Cultivating a Spirit of Inquiry and Curiosity

Continuing the legacy of exploration also means fostering a culture of inquiry and curiosity. The treasure hunt was built on the premise of asking questions—questions about history, about the meaning of clues, and about the world itself. The hunt encouraged participants to dig deeper, to think critically, and to question what they thought they knew. This process of inquiry is at the heart of all great discoveries. Whether we're exploring the natural world, scientific theories, or even the complexities of human nature, inquiry is the first step toward new understanding.

In today's fast-paced, technology-driven world, it's easy to become distracted or complacent. But the pursuit of knowledge and discovery should always remain at the forefront. Encouraging people to ask questions, to challenge the status quo, and to dig deeper into subjects that fascinate them is a key part of continuing the legacy of exploration. It is through this curiosity and hunger for answers that progress is made, new innovations are born, and the world is forever changed.

3. Embracing the Challenges of Exploration

Exploration is rarely a smooth journey. The treasure hunt itself was filled with obstacles—riddles that were difficult to solve, locations that were hard to pinpoint, and moments of doubt when success seemed elusive. But it was precisely these challenges that made the journey so rewarding. To truly embrace the legacy of exploration, we must also embrace the inevitable challenges and setbacks that come with it. It is often through adversity that we learn the most about ourselves and the world around us.

As we move forward, it is important to view challenges as opportunities for growth rather than roadblocks to success. Every difficult moment, every puzzle that doesn't have an immediate answer, is an invitation to think creatively, to adapt, and to persevere. By encouraging future explorers to embrace challenges with resilience and a positive mindset, we ensure that the legacy of exploration will live on. It's not about avoiding obstacles but about learning how to navigate them with confidence and determination.

4. The Role of Technology in Modern Exploration

While exploration may traditionally have been associated with physical journeys to unknown lands, today's explorers are not just venturing into the physical world—they are venturing into the digital realm, the realms of space, and the very depths of human knowledge. Technology plays an increasingly important role in modern exploration, providing tools that allow us to uncover new territories, unlock new insights, and connect with people and information in ways that were once unimaginable.

From mapping the human genome to exploring distant planets, technology enables us to push the boundaries of what is possible. As we look to the future of exploration, we must continue to embrace these technological advancements, using them to enhance our understanding of the world and the universe. The treasure hunt has shown how technology can be used to create interactive, immersive experiences that engage and challenge participants. Moving forward, we should encourage future explorers to not only take advantage of the tools available but to innovate, creating new ways to explore both the physical and digital worlds.

5. Building a Community of Explorers

Another key element in continuing the legacy of exploration is building a supportive community of like-minded individuals. The treasure hunt, while a solitary pursuit in some respects, also fostered a sense of camaraderie among participants. Whether they were working together to solve a particularly challenging clue or exchanging theories and ideas, the sense of community was integral to the journey.

In the same way, the legacy of exploration can be carried forward by cultivating a global community of explorers. By connecting people with a shared passion for discovery, we can create a network of individuals who encourage one another, collaborate, and inspire each other to take on new challenges. This community can extend beyond the realm of treasure hunting to encompass a wide array of fields— science, history, art, technology, and beyond. The more we come together to share our knowledge and experiences, the more we enrich the process of exploration and increase its impact on the world.

6. Leaving a Lasting Impact

Finally, the most important aspect of continuing the legacy of exploration is ensuring that the knowledge and discoveries made along the way are not forgotten. Every explorer contributes to a larger body of knowledge that can be passed on to future generations. As this treasure hunt shows, the value of exploration extends beyond the individual; it is about leaving a mark on the world that others can build upon.

To continue the legacy of exploration, we must ensure that the knowledge gained during the hunt is shared and preserved. This could mean documenting the journey, recording the lessons learned, and making the discoveries available to others. It's about creating a foundation for future explorers to stand upon, giving them the tools, the inspiration, and the knowledge they need to continue the work.

The treasure hunt may be coming to an end, but the legacy of exploration is far from over. By inspiring the next generation of explorers, cultivating curiosity, embracing challenges, leveraging technology, building communities, and leaving a lasting impact, we ensure that the spirit of exploration continues to thrive. The true value of the hunt lies not just in the treasures found, but in the spark of curiosity it ignites and the future it sets in motion. As we look ahead, we must continue to dream, to explore, and to uncover the mysteries of the world. The legacy of exploration is alive and well, and it is up to all of us to carry the torch forward.

How You Can Inspire Others

In the wake of completing a treasure hunt as grand as the one described in this book, it becomes evident that the true value of such an adventure lies not just in the treasures that are unearthed, but in the potential it has to inspire others. The journey is far from a solitary endeavor. It is a shared experience, a catalyst for igniting the spark of curiosity, creativity, and exploration in the hearts of others. The question then becomes: how can you, as a participant or as someone inspired by this adventure, inspire others to embark on their own quests, take risks, and embrace the pursuit of discovery?

The path forward is not only about continuing the journey of exploration but also about enabling others to feel empowered to embark on their own adventures. By sharing knowledge, encouraging exploration, and embracing the principles that define the spirit of discovery, you can become a beacon of inspiration for others.

1. Sharing Your Journey: The Power of Storytelling

One of the most effective ways to inspire others is through the power of storytelling. Humans are naturally drawn to stories—they help us connect, reflect, and understand. If you've participated in a treasure hunt or have experienced the joy of discovery, share your story. Talk about the challenges you faced, the lessons you learned, and the sense of accomplishment you gained when solving the riddles or uncovering hidden treasures.

Your story doesn't just have to be about the end result—it can also include the emotional highs and lows of the journey. The struggles, frustrations, and moments of self-doubt are just as important as the triumphs. By sharing both the successes and the setbacks, you give others the confidence to persevere when faced with their own challenges. Your story could serve as a roadmap for others to follow, showing them that the journey is just as important as the destination and that every twist and turn has something valuable to teach.

Storytelling can happen in various forms—whether through social media posts, blogs, podcasts, or even casual conversations with friends and family. The key is to make your journey relatable and accessible, allowing others to see themselves in your story. This can open doors for those who may have never considered taking on a challenge or venturing into the unknown.

2. Be a Mentor or Guide

Inspiring others doesn't always mean starting from scratch or creating your own treasure hunt. One of the most impactful ways to inspire others is by becoming a mentor or guide for those who are just starting their own journeys. Share your knowledge and experience with people who are eager to learn, offering advice, encouragement, and resources that will help them succeed.

Mentorship can take many forms—whether it's providing guidance on how to approach a specific challenge or helping someone develop the mindset and strategies they need to tackle obstacles. If you've been through a treasure hunt or a challenging project, offer your wisdom to those who are navigating their own adventures. Even if you don't have all the answers, your experience can be an invaluable resource.

Mentoring is about more than just giving advice—it's about showing others that they are capable of achieving their own goals. Sometimes, all someone needs is the encouragement to take the first step. By being a supportive presence, you empower others to move forward with confidence and determination.

3. Encourage Exploration Beyond the Known

The treasure hunt illustrated that exploration isn't limited to physical locations; it can also extend to new ways of thinking, uncharted ideas, and personal growth. Encourage those around you to explore beyond the confines of their comfort zones. Whether it's trying out a new hobby, learning a new skill, or diving into a subject that seems daunting, exploration is about challenging oneself to step into the unknown and expand one's horizons.

Invite others to embrace the spirit of exploration in everyday life. You don't need a treasure chest or a mysterious map to spark curiosity. A simple invitation to read a book on an unfamiliar topic, participate in a creative challenge, or explore new places—even locally—can ignite the desire to discover. Encourage them to ask questions, to challenge conventional wisdom, and to seek out experiences that will push their limits.

The beauty of exploration is that it's not confined to a particular field or discipline. It's a mindset that encourages people to approach life with open-mindedness, creativity, and a willingness to learn. Encourage others to think of exploration as an ongoing process—a continuous journey rather than a destination. It's about embracing change, being curious, and constantly striving for growth.

4. Lead by Example: Show the Power of Persistence

One of the most profound ways you can inspire others is by leading by example. The treasure hunt, like many journeys in life, is not without its challenges. The path to discovery requires persistence, determination, and the ability to keep going even when things don't go as planned. By demonstrating perseverance, you show others the value of sticking with a goal, even when the road ahead seems difficult.

When you face challenges in your own life—whether personal, professional, or creative—let others see how you handle them. Show them that failure is not something to be feared, but rather an opportunity to learn and grow. By embracing setbacks as part of the journey and refusing to give up, you model resilience for others.

You can also show others that success is often the result of consistent effort over time. The treasure hunt was a five-year project, and much like any ambitious goal, it didn't happen overnight. By taking small steps toward a larger goal and maintaining focus, you demonstrate how persistence can yield extraordinary results.

5. Create Opportunities for Others to Engage

To inspire others, sometimes you need to create the space for them to engage and experience the excitement of exploration firsthand. You don't have to create an elaborate treasure hunt to do so—there are many ways to open doors for others to join in on a journey of discovery.

Consider organizing local challenges, scavenger hunts, or collaborative projects that encourage others to participate in the joy of discovery. Host an event, create a community, or simply extend an invitation to those around you to join you in exploring something new. Whether it's a historical walk, a creative puzzle-solving evening, or an online exploration of a specific topic, offering opportunities for hands-on engagement is one of the most powerful ways to inspire action.

Creating opportunities for others to get involved is about making exploration accessible to everyone. Not everyone will be ready to embark on a grand adventure, but small steps—such as discovering a local hidden gem or solving a simple riddle—can spark the desire for more. By providing these opportunities, you ignite curiosity in others and create a culture of discovery that can spread far and wide.

6. Celebrate the Journey and the Learning Process

Lastly, it's essential to emphasize that inspiration comes not just from the end goal, but from the journey itself. Acknowledge the small wins, the milestones, and the lessons learned along the way. Celebrate the process of discovery—whether it's finding a clue, solving a puzzle, or learning something new about yourself. By highlighting the value of the journey and the personal growth that comes with it, you help others recognize that exploration is not only about the destination but also about the transformation that takes place along the way.

When you share your excitement for the journey, you show others that the process of learning, solving problems, and pushing past challenges is just as rewarding as reaching the finish line. It's the lessons gained from every step that make the experience truly invaluable.

Inspiring others to embrace the spirit of exploration is about more than just sharing a treasure hunt—it's about creating a mindset, a way of thinking that encourages curiosity, creativity, and persistence. By telling your story, mentoring others, encouraging exploration, leading by example, creating opportunities, and celebrating the learning process, you can help others find their own path to discovery. As the legacy of this treasure hunt continues to unfold, the most important thing is that the spirit of exploration lives on in those who are inspired to follow their own journeys, discover new treasures, and share their findings with the world.

Made in the USA
Las Vegas, NV
02 December 2024

13218425R00070